BUSINESS INTERACTION
Presentation

지은이	윤주영
펴낸이	윤주영
펴낸곳	HiEnglish
펴낸날	2017년 11월 30일 초판 1쇄 발행
참여자	서정민, Bruce Alexander
디자인	정희정

전화	(02) 335 1002
팩스	(02) 6499 0219
주소	서울 마포구 홍익로5안길 8
홈페이지	www.hienglish.com
이메일	broadcast1@hienglish.com
등록번호	제2005-000040호
ISBN	979-11-85342-32-0
Copyright	ⓒ 2017 HiEnglish
정가	17,000원

All rights reserved. No part of this publication may be reproduced, stored in a retrieval system, or transmitted in any form or by any means, electronic, mechanical, photocopying, recording, or otherwise, without the prior permission of the publisher.

Preface

Business Interacion 시리즈는 국내 대기업 및 대학에서 비즈니스 영어 교육용 교재로 많은 사랑을 받았던 비즈니스잉글리시 케첩 시리즈의 개정판입니다.

이 책은 글로벌 시대에 딱 맞는 커뮤니케이션 능력을 향상시킬 수 있도록 제작되었습니다. 다양한 비즈니스 환경에서 외국 오너들과 자신 있게 협력하고 의사소통할 수 있도록 실무에 자주 사용하는 표현과 어휘를 중심으로 구성하였으며 읽고, 듣고, 쓰고 말하는 능력을 키울 수 있는 기회를 제공합니다. 또한 비즈니스 환경에서 반드시 알아야 할 표현(expressions)과 어휘(vocabulary)를 소개하고 있으며 회화, roleplay, 연습 문제 등을 통해 내용을 확실히 익힐 수 있도록 합니다.

Business Interacion은 Presentation, Meeting, Email 총 3권으로 구성되어 있습니다. Presentation에서는 영어로 프레젠테이션을 매끄럽게 발표하는데 도움을 받을 수 있습니다. Meeting에서는 외국 파트너들과 효과적인 회의를 진행하기 위해 필요한 표현과 어휘를, Email에서는 직장에서 자주 쓰는 이메일, 회의록, 계약서 작성하는 방법에 대해 배울 수 있습니다. 그리고 QR 코드를 찍어 영상을 보면서 재미있고, 다양하게 학습할 수 있도록 구성했습니다. 본 시리즈는 무엇보다도 외국인들이 실제로 쓰는 생생한 표현들을 많이 포함하고 있습니다. 표현과 어휘를 중심으로 연습하면 오늘날 필요로 하는 글로벌 인재로 성장하는데 많은 도움이 될 것이라 확신합니다.

2017년 11월
윤주영

Contents

Unit 01	**Starting the Presentation**	7
Unit 02	**Engaging the Audience**	15
Unit 03	**Stating the Purpose**	23
Unit 04	**Outlining**	31
Unit 05	**Actual Case 1** Got a Meeting? Take a Walk	39
Unit 06	**Analyzing**	45
Unit 07	**Making Comparisons**	53
Unit 08	**Making Contrasts**	61
Unit 09	**Emphasizing**	69
Unit 10	**Actual Case 2** The Jobs We'll Lose to Machines – and the Ones We Won't	77
Unit 11	**Introducing Visuals**	83

Unit 12	Describing a Bar Graph	91
Unit 13	Describing a Line Graph	99
Unit 14	Describing a Pie Chart	107
Unit 15	Actual Case 3 Art of the Interface	115
Unit 16	Highlighting Information	121
Unit 17	Summarizing the Main Points	129
Unit 18	Closing a Presentation	137
Unit 19	Handling the Q&A Session	145
Unit 20	Actual Case 4 Future of Work and Learning	153
Answer Key		159

Unit 01

Starting the Presentation

 Warm-up

1. Based on your experience in giving presentations, have you ever made such a good impression at the beginning immediately captured the audience's attention? If so, how did you start?

2. Can you think of some specific attitudes which might give a good or bad impression, especially when giving presentations? Share your ideas with the class.

01 Vocabulary

A Word Definition
Underline the word with the given definition.

1 to produce a result, answer, or piece of information

   My investment <u>yields</u> about $2,000 a year in profits.

2 giving you hope and confidence

   A recent experiment has shown <u>encouraging</u> results.

3 not definite or certain, because you may want to change things

   I'll send you a <u>tentative</u> schedule for the interviews.

4 happening before something that is more important, often in order to prepare for it

   The project is still in its <u>preliminary</u> stages.

B Word Use
Write your own sentence using the underlined word in the sentence.

1 The topic of the workshop is how to improve **company-wide** communication.

   _____

2 Tickets are available both **on site** and online.

   _____

3 Properly identifying the **target audience** is essential in planning an advertising campaign.

   _____

4 Technological advances **in the last decade** have totally transformed the media landscape.

   _____

02 Expression

A Key Expressions

1 It gives me great pleasure to
- It gives me great pleasure to welcome you today.
- It's my pleasure to open this year's sales conference.

2 you've all made it
- I'm so glad that you've all made it from our offices around the world.
- I'm delighted that you've all made it to this event.

3 on such (a) short notice
- I'm pleased that you've all made it to this meeting on such (a) short notice.
- Thanks for gathering on such (a) short notice.

4 give you a general overview of
- I'm going to spend some time today giving you a general overview of our security problems.
- I'll give you a general overview of our new product by listing its main features.

5 I'll be very brief
- This will be a quick meeting so I'll be very brief.
- I'll be very brief as I know it's quite late.

6 start off with
- I'd like to start off with some updates on our sales figures.
- I want to start off with a couple of questions.

7 update you on
- I'd like to update you on our recent technological advancements.
- I'm very pleased to have a chance to update you on our ongoing projects.

8 I tell you
- Now, I tell you, this sounds like a new idea that is well worth debating.
- I tell you what, why don't we start off with something interesting to talk about?

03 Presentation (1)

A What's the presentation about?

_____

_____

B Summarize the story and present it to the class.

_____

_____

_____

_____

C Complete the sentences with the phrases in the box.

- start off   • on site   • made it   • welcome to

(1)_____ Optium Conference 2016. I'm glad you've all (2)_____ to today's conference on such short notice. I am thrilled to present a totally new style of tablet for you. However, before I begin my presentation, I want to (3)_____ with some stats about the conference. There are over 1,000 attendees here today. This may be the biggest product launch in Optium's history–I'm not sure, but I know it's the largest in the last decade, so it's very special day! There are developers here from over 32 countries, including Japan and Germany, and we've got some great stuff for your businesses. There will be over 60 lab sessions-and of those, 22 are hands-on, where you'll going to sit in front of the machines during the sessions-as well as 80 presentation sessions. What's more, over 300 Optium engineers are going to be (4)_____ this week to help you.

04 Presentation (2)

Give a presentation for five minutes using the slide below.

You are going to begin a conference by welcoming the audience. This is one of the largest global conferences in the IT field. A lot of distinguished developers and engineers are in attendance. You will introduce yourself and this conference with the information on the second slide.

Strategic Analysis

- **The Vision**
  To make search engines so powerful they can understand "everything in the world"

- **The Mission**
  To organize the world's information and make it universally accessible and useful

- **The Focus**
  To continue to focus on innovation and on the user experience

UNIT 01 Starting the Presentation

05 Sample Presentation

Read the script below aloud with proper rhythm and pronunciation.

> Hi, my name is Nick and I'm a researcher here at AMT Labs. It gives me great pleasure to welcome you to this conference. I hope you are all having a good time. I'm here today to talk about strategic analysis.
>
> I'm sure it's everyone's favorite discussion topic. But, we promise over the next 30 minutes you will learn a lot and might even have a little fun. We'll first analyze different corporations in the IT industry. We'll start off with Google. Let me first introduce their vision, mission and focus.
>
> First, their vision is to make search engines so powerful they can "understand everything in the world." Pretty powerful stuff there, right? Meanwhile, their mission is to organize the world's information and make it universally accessible and useful. Hmm, is that even possible? And lastly, their focus is on innovation and user experience. Isn't everybody's?

Presentation Tip

Start Strong

You've heard it before: First impressions are powerful. Believe it. The first 2-3 minutes of the presentation are the most important. The audience wants to like you and they will give you a few minutes at the beginning to engage them — don't miss the opportunity. Most presenters fail here because they ramble on too long about superfluous background information, their personal/professional history, etc.

06 Mr. Q's Presentation

🎧 **Listen to Mr. Q's presentation and answer the questions below.**

1. What most likely is Mr. Q's job?

   ⓐ Product developer ⓑ Customer service representative

   ⓒ Advertising agent ⓓ Personnel manager

2. What is Mr. Q's presentation mainly about?

   ⓐ Excessive business expenses ⓑ Construction of a new building

   ⓒ An advertising campaign ⓓ A project update

3. What will the audience probably do next?

   _____

   _____

   _____

BUSINESS JOKES

A major speaker for the annual auto dealers convention was visiting the rest room just before he was to speak to the 10,000 members.
He was asked, "Are you our special speaker?"
"Yes, I sure am and I am excited to be here," he replied.
"Are you nervous?" "No, I'm never nervous before I give a big speech." "If you are not nervous, then what are you doing in the ladies room?"

UNIT 01 Starting the Presentation

07 Exercise

A Underline the best word to complete each sentence.

1 I'll give you a general (overview / overvalue) of our new product by listing its main features.

2 Our technicians will be available (onside / on site) 24 hours a day to assist you.

B Fill in the blanks with the given words.

| • notice | • brief | • company-wide |
| • start off | • target | • encouraging |

1 A preliminary field test has yielded some _____ results.

2 I'll be very _____ as I know it's very late.

3 Thank you for attending our _____ product review.

4 I'd like to _____ with some updates on our sales figures.

C Fill in the blanks with the given words.

- is essential when delivering a speech
- have transformed the market fundamentally
- on such short notice
- in its preliminary stage

1 Technological advances in the last decade _____.

2 The project is still _____.

3 Properly identifying the target audience _____.

4 I'm pleased that you've all made it to this meeting _____.

Unit 02

Engaging the Audience

 **Warm-up**

1 Do you have your own ways to grab the audience's interest for your presentation? What do you usually do?

2 It is really important to build a good rapport and evoke the audience's sympathy to achieve the maximum effect of a presentation. What do you usually use to make it effective?

01 Vocabulary

A Word Definition

Underline the word with the given definition.

1 a sudden, dramatic, and important discovery or development

 This research could be the biggest breakthrough in cancer treatment of our generation.

2 reasonable and likely to be true or successful

 That isn't a plausible excuse for being late.

3 to taste food or drink in order to see what it is like

 Of the two beverages that were sampled, testers unanimously preferred the sweeter one.

4 making you feel a desire to have or do something

 I can't resist the tantalizing cookies cooling on the table.

B Word Use

Write your own sentence using the underlined word in the sentence.

1 The government has **indulged in** widespread corruption.

 _____

2 My new job is to **pass on** all relevant information to our potential clients.

 _____

3 Asahi made the best **brew** using many secret ingredients.

 _____

4 The latest Samsung smartphone has **mind-blowing** features.

 _____

02 Expression

A Key Expressions

1 be of particular interest to
- This internship program will be of particular interest to students who desire to be international lawyers.
- This course seems to be of particular interest to CPAs.

2 My topic is particularly relevant to
- My topic is particularly relevant to the current economic situation in Korea.
- My topic is particularly relevant to those of you who just retired.

3 By the end of this talk, you'll be familiar with
- By the end of this talk, you'll be familiar with ancient Korean history.
- By the end of this talk, you'll be familiar with the new banking systems in the U.S.

4 change the entire industry
- JMP Entertainment has been changing the entire music industry.
- You can change the entire industry with a simple, powerful idea.

5 transform the landscape
- The new law began to transform the political landscape.
- The global financial crisis will eventually transform the world's financial landscape.

6 words alone cannot express
- Words alone cannot express how much my coworkers have inspired me.
- Words alone cannot express the gratitude I have for my staff.

7 add to our already extensive list of
- Reading this book will add to your already extensive list of vocabulary.
- We will add this new technology to our already extensive list of patents.

8 all the ins and outs of
- I don't really understand all the ins and outs of politics.
- This chart illustrates all the ins and outs of the European financial market.

03 Presentation (1)

A What's the presentation about?

_____
_____

B Summarize the story and present it to the class.

_____
_____
_____
_____

C Complete the sentences with the phrases in the box.

> · familiar   · introduced   · without   · revolutionary

In 1986, we introduced our first product, which we called Maxio. It changed the whole computer industry. In 2002, we (1)_____ the first digital camera, the Maxcoder. It changed the entire photography industry. By the end of this talk, you'll be (2)_____ with our newest product which will transform the social media landscape.

See, today we are introducing three (3)_____ features. The first one is a wider screen with a photo viewer. The second is an innovative mobile phone. The size is smaller than before but it is much more powerful than previous generations. And the third is our totally redesigned software, something you might call a breakthrough in mobile communications. You can access the Internet anywhere (4)_____ rapidly exhausting your batteries. This new product is called the MaxMac!

04 Presentation (2)

Give a presentation for five minutes using the slide below.

Your company is a nation-wide beer supplier; you have just received a mind-blowing new brew. You are going to introduce it to your clients. Before that, you need to capture the clients' attention. Use the following slide and make up your own story to engage the audience.

So you might be asking yourself…

How is somthing as magical & Wonderous as beer created?

05 Sample Presentation

Read the script below aloud with proper rhythm and pronunciation.

> Good morning everyone. I'm glad to see so many of you could join us this morning. We have something very special and exciting to share with you today. As you know, it is not very often that a new brew is released, that is why I had to invite you here today to introduce to you the latest brew that we are adding to our already extensive list of products.
>
> The main reason we wanted you to attend in person is so that you would have the opportunity to taste this amazing brew for yourselves, because words alone cannot express how mind-blowing and wonderful this next generation of beer actually tastes. You need to taste it to believe it. I'm sure you will find that you have never tasted anything like it before and I know you will be asking yourselves how something this magical could be created. So without further ado, I present to you the tantalizing Regency Beer. I hope you enjoy it as much as we have enjoyed producing it.

Presentation Tip

Show Your Passion

If I had only one tip to give, it would be to be passionate about your topic and let that enthusiasm come out. You need great content and professional, well-designed visuals. But it is all for naught if you do not have a deep, heartfelt belief in your topic. The biggest item that separates mediocre presenters from world class ones is the ability to connect with an audience in an honest and exciting way. Don't hold back. And let your passion for your topic come out for all to see.

06 Mr. Q's Presentation

🎧 **Listen to Mr. Q's presentation and answer the questions below.**

1 Who should be interested in Mr. Q's presentation?

    ⓐ Soda makers   ⓑ Juice vendors

    ⓒ Beer retailers   ⓓ Local brewers

2 According to the speaker, how should the new brew be promoted?

    ⓐ Through TV advertising   ⓑ Through sampling events

    ⓒ Through social media   ⓓ Through flyers

3 What do you think the main purpose of Mr. Q's presentation is?

_____

_____

_____

BUSINESS JOKES

The candidate was interviewing for a job at a phone answer center and was asked to make a sentence using the words Yellow, Pink, and Green. After thinking about it for a couple of minutes, her reply was, "When the phone goes GREEN, GREEN, GREEN, I PINK up the phone and say YELLOW!"
She got the job.

UNIT 02 Engaging the Audience

07 Exercise

A Underline the best word to complete each sentence.

1 Dean is talking about how to (transact / **transform**) the landscape of e-commerce with the new technology.

2 This article covers several tips on enjoying a better (**brew** / breed) at home.

B Fill in the blanks with the given words.

| • tantalizing | • indulge | • entire |
| • plausible | • revolutionary | • breakthrough |

1 Civil servants must not _____ in any acts of injustice or corruption.

2 When Amy looked at the _____ dishes people were having at the next table, she suddenly became even hungrier.

3 Julie got reprimanded because she could not give her boss a _____ explanation for her frequent tardiness to work.

4 IT experts expect a large _____ in wireless communication in the near future.

C Fill in the blanks with the given words.

- you'll be familiar with
- words alone cannot express
- this program will be of particular interest
- changing the entire industry

1 _____ to teachers who rely heavily on textbooks.

2 By the end of this talk, _____ all the new models of this season.

3 A couple of social networking programs are _____.

4 _____ how scary that movie was. Words alone cannot express how scary that movie was.

Unit 03

Stating the Purpose

 Warm-up

1. Which do you think is a better way of stating the purpose of a presentation; stating the purpose of the presentation directly, or using a dramatic story or anecdote? Share the reason for your preference.

2. What kind of strong is most effective? What anecdotes should you avoid at all cost? why?

01 Vocabulary

A Word Definition
Underline the word with the given definition.

1 to not do something that you want to do

The building manager asked us to refrain from making noise.

2 relating to the most basic and important parts of something

There is a fundamental cultural difference between the two archrivals Samsung Electronics and LG Electronics.

3 not likely to cause any arguments or disagreements

The board of directors went to a lot of effort to appoint a noncontroversial CEO.

4 showing strong positive feelings about an activity and determination to succeed at it

The former New York mayor was ardent in his support of the online privacy bill.

B Word Use
Write your own sentence using the underlined word in the sentence.

1 We will **set forth** our strategy in three parts: research, implementation and results.

_____

2 Our online postgraduate programs **cater to** the needs of full-time workers with busy schedules.

_____

3 Agendas should be well planned in order to cover all points as the meeting **unfolds**.

_____

4 No one but James managed to **come up with** a new idea for reducing expenses.

_____

02 Expression

A Key Expressions

1 allow me to open by –ing
- Please allow me to open by talking about the most tragic accident in our history.
- Please allow me to open by making a close observation.

2 The objective of this presentation is to
- The objective of this presentation is to give more information on our marketing strategies to our new employees.
- The objective of this presentation is to influence and inspire our sales representatives.

3 What I'd like to inform you of is
- What I'd like to inform you of is that we have achieved our sales goal for this year.
- What I'd like to inform you of is that the deadline for submitting works to the exhibition has been extended to March 31, 2018.

4 This presentation will outline
- This presentation will outline our plans to launch a new advertising campaign.
- This presentation will outline the recently proposed housing regulations.

5 I would like to present to you
- I would like to present to you our new hardware and software products.
- I would like to present to you our new and exciting website.

6 bring ... to your attention
- I would like to bring the latest issues to your attention.
- I need to bring to your attention that our deadline has been extended until April 15.

7 It is our mission to
- It is our mission to manufacture and sell quality home appliances.
- It is our mission to care for your pet as if it were our own.

8 This won't take more than
- This won't take more than a day or two.
- This probably won't take more than 40 minutes.

UNIT 03 Stating the Purpose 25

03 Presentation (1)

A What's the presentation about?

_____
_____

B Summarize the story and present it to the class.

_____
_____
_____
_____

C Complete the sentences with the phrases in the box.

> · hopefully   · potential   · morality   · implications

Please allow me to open by saying that I don't want to talk today about the (1)_____ of capital punishment. For this presentation, I would like to present to you death penalty cases in a unique way that is (2)_____ noncontroversial. By the way this won't take more than 20 minutes.

Before I do that, over the course of a few minutes I want to tell you how a death penalty case unfolds. I would also like to talk about its (3)_____ and realities. Basically there are four stages in a death penalty case. I'll go over them one by one for you. And then I would like to bring (4)_____ problems to your attention.

04 Presentation (2)

Give a presentation for five minutes using the slide below.

You are going to give a presentation concerning statistical data about Face.com users all over the world, especially users in Western Europe. Some countries such as the UK, France, and Italy showed a remarkable number of active users. With this data research, your company will develop a new marketing strategy.

UNIT 03 Stating the Purpose

05 Sample Presentation

Read the script below aloud with proper rhythm and pronunciation.

Good day everybody, and welcome. I plan to be brief, so if you have any questions, please refrain from interrupting me. We will have a ten-minute Q&A at the end of the presentation. The objective of this presentation is to inform you that MQ Marketing Strategies has just secured a contract to develop a new marketing strategy for Face.com. As you are aware, they are one of the leading social network providers in the world. It is our mission to come up with a marketing campaign that will specifically target users in Western Europe but also apply to users worldwide. This presentation will outline the fundamental needs and the tools required to ensure a smooth and successful marketing campaign which would benefit both Face.com and MQ Marketing Strategies. We will set forth our strategy in three parts: research, implementation and results. I also need to bring to your attention that our deadline is exactly three months from today so I expect you to be on your best game.

Presentation Tip

Word Summary

Can you summarize your idea in fifteen words? If not, rewrite it and try again. Speaking is an inefficient medium for communicating information: so you should know what the important fifteen words are so they can be repeated.

06 Mr. Q's Presentation

🎧 **Listen to Mr. Q's presentation and answer the questions below.**

1 How does Mr. Q open the presentation?

    ⓐ By introducing himself   ⓑ By demonstrating a product

    ⓒ By talking about the weather   ⓓ By thanking the audience

2 How does Mr. Q describe his marketing plan?

    ⓐ Well-funded   ⓑ Eye catching

    ⓒ Unique   ⓓ Cost effective

3 Do you think Mr. Q stated the purpose of his presentation effectively? Why or why not?

_____

_____

_____

BUSINESS JOKES

A businessman checked into a hotel and, because he was concerned that the dining room might close soon, left his luggage at the front desk and went immediately to eat. After a leisurely dinner, he realized that he had forgotten his room number. He went back to the desk and told the clerk on duty, "My name is Henry Davis, can you please tell me what room I am in?"
"Certainly," said the clerk. "You're in the lobby."

07 Exercise

A Underline the best word to complete each sentence.

1. How did you (come / make) up with such a brilliant idea?
2. The new CEO has promised to make a (fundamental / elementary) change in our organization.

B Fill in the blanks with the given words.

- encourage
- objective
- ardent
- unfold
- preliminary
- refrain

1. Please _____ from making noises during the movie.
2. You should double check your schedule to make sure that your business travel plans _____ smoothly.
3. I was an _____ fan of the works of James Garner in college.
4. The _____ of this presentation is to describe preliminary findings from case

C Fill in the blanks with the given words.

- it is our mission to encourage
- this presentation will outline
- if there is something I should know about
- this won't take more than half an hour

1. _____ please bring it to my attention.
2. As teachers, _____ as many students as possible.
3. _____, and I'll take questions afterwards.
4. _____ our plans to expand our services into China.

Unit 04

Outlining

 Warm-up

1. What parts are normally included in the outline of the presentation? Which parts do you usually include for your presentation?
2. The purpose will decide what type of structure you should use for your presentation; logical vs chronological structure. Based on to your experience, which type do you prefer? Why?

01 Vocabulary

A Word Definition

Underline the word with the given definition.

1 directly relating to something that is being considered

Do you think it is pertinent for me to cite those facts?

2 extremely large

I am fortunate that I have been getting a vast amount of experience in such a short time.

3 very determined to succeed or get what you want

It is seriously frustrating to deal with aggressive sales people visiting offices without prior appointments.

4 to define again or differently

We need to redefine our marketing strategy to survive in this intensely competitive market.

B Word Use

Write your own sentence using the underlined word in the sentence.

1 South Korea has made a **remarkable** recovery from the great economic crisis of 1997.

_____

2 It **occurred** to me that Rachel told me she moved to a new company, LINE.

_____

3 It is supposed to be the best savings account for **all age brackets**.

_____

4 We have to **triple** sales in just two months to avoid a financial crisis.

_____

02 Expression

A Key Expressions

1 in my presentation, I will share [discuss, focus on]
- In my presentation, I will share the results of this new plant construction project.
- In my presentation, I will discuss how to work efficiently and effectively.

2 I've divided my talk into
- I've divided my talk into three major parts: vision, strategy and outcome.
- Today I've divided my presentation into two important areas, politics and the economy.

3 Point one deals with ..., point two ..., and point three ...
- Point one deals with the issue of pay raises, point two describes working conditions and point three talks about the difficulties in creating new jobs.
- Point one deals with common grammatical mistakes, point two describes essay writing strategies, and point three talks about useful expressions in business English.

4 Let me begin by emphasizing ..., then, I'll move on to .... After that ...
- Let me begin by emphasizing what is really happening now, then, I'll move on to what to do about it. After that, we will have lunch.
- Let me begin by emphasizing what Ms. Toledo has done for us, then, I'll move on to who she is and why she is here. After that we will meet her on stage.

5 go into more detail about
- I would like to go into more detail about the current financial situation in Greece.
- I would like to go into more detail about the term, "postmodernism" used in the textbook.

6 elaborate on each one in much greater detail
- I will be able to elaborate on each one in much greater detail, if needed.
- He has to elaborate on each one in much greater detail for the law school students to prepare for the national bar exam at the end of this month.

7 set aside 20 minutes for questions
- Just to remind you, I set aside 20 minutes for questions.
- You should make sure that Mr. Tate sets aside 10 minutes for questions.

8 keep your questions to the end
- Don't forget to keep your questions to the end.
- For the interview this afternoon, you need to keep your questions to the end.

03 Presentation (1)

A What's the presentation about?

_____
_____

B Summarize the story and present it to the class.

_____
_____
_____
_____

C Complete the sentences with the phrases in the box.

> · innovative   · spread   · divided   · aside

In my presentation today, I will discuss how to think of a new idea and (1)_____ keywords about it across the world. I've (2)_____ my talk into three parts. They show how a company called Silk tripled their sales while making a simple but (3)_____ device, how an athlete named Jeff Koons became a legend within a few short years, and how Frank Gehry redefined what we now call the telephone.

You are probably wondering what "Sauce" is. It happened to be the title of a cookbook I wrote five years ago. It was not only about sauces but also about other types of food, and sold pretty well. Each part won't take more than 5 minutes. I've set (4)_____ 20 minutes for questions at the end of my presentation. So, I would appreciate it if you could you keep your questions to the end.

04 Presentation (2)

Give a presentation for five minutes using the slide below.

You are going to introduce a remarkable new strategy for mobile marketing to your client. You need reliable data and research as proof. You will give a presentation based on an outline on the following slide.

Overview

What? Mobile Landscape
- Device, platforms and operations

When? Mobile Usage
- Browsing and Apps
- Multi-channel engagement

Who? Brands and Service Engagement

How? Reaching a Mobile Audience
- Interation methods
- Advertising and response mechanisms

_____
_____
_____
_____
_____
_____
_____

05 Sample Presentation

Read the script below aloud with proper rhythm and pronunciation.

Good day to all of you and thank you for the opportunity to present to you this morning. When preparing for this presentation it occurred to me that we have to ask ourselves four very important and pertinent questions. What? When? Who? And how? I have therefore divided my talk into four main points and, by doing so, I will elaborate on each one in much greater detail. If you have any questions, feel free to interrupt me at any time. Let me begin by emphasizing that mobile marketing has fast become one of the leading ways to advertise one's product. We now have the means to ensure that your campaign can reach millions of viewers by just a few taps on a cell phone screen and, after extensive research, we have put together a vast amount of data to support this model. I would like to go into more details about each of these points at this time.

Presentation Tip

Keep it Simple

When planning your presentation, you should always keep in mind the question: What is the key message for my audience to take away? You should be able to communicate that key message very briefly. Some experts recommend that you can write it on the back of a business card, or say it in no more than 15 words. Whichever rule you choose, the important thing is to keep your core message focused and brief.

06 Mr. Q's Presentation

🎧 **Listen to Mr. Q's presentation and answer the questions below.**

1 1. What is the topic of Mr. Q's presentation?

ⓐ Book marketing ⓑ Mobile marketing

ⓒ Wise investing ⓓ Hotel booking

2 What does Mr. Q say specify who need to be in their marketing approach?

ⓐ Confident ⓑ Smart

ⓒ Aggressive ⓓ Careful

3 How does Mr. Q outline his presentation?

_____

_____

_____

BUSINESS JOKES	At a meeting, the corporate manager told a joke. Everyone on the team laughed except one guy. The manager asked him, "Didn't you understand my joke?" The guy replied, "Oh, I understood it, but I resigned yesterday."

UNIT 04 Outlining

07 Exercise

A Underline the best word to complete each sentence.

1 In my presentation, I will (focus / develop) on organic firms that opened between 2015 and 2017.

2 The company is carrying out an (regressive / aggressive) marketing campaign in order to increase its market share.

B Fill in the blanks with the given words.

- triple
- leading
- divide
- pertinent
- remarkable
- redefine

1 Employees should make every effort to _____ their roles to become more involved.

2 Do you really believe you can _____ sales in just six months in this sluggish economy?

3 Mr. Taylor's new book seems _____ to both today's consumers and producers.

4 The semiconductor industry as a whole has achieved _____ growth in the last six months.

C Fill in the blanks with the given words.

- to focus on the details
- point one deals with the shoplifting issue
- go into more detail about
- please keep your questions to the end

1 Questions in the middle of the presentation can be disrupting, so _____.

2 _____, point two describes the damage to our profits, and point three talks about possible solutions.

3 I've divided my talk into smaller topics _____.

4 Professor Lee will _____ social communication skills tomorrow.

Unit 05 Actual Case 1

Got a Meeting? Take a Walk

Nilofer Merchant

Nilofer Merchant suggests a small idea that just might have a big impact on your life and health: Next time you have a one-on-one meeting, make it into a "walking meeting" - and let ideas flow while you walk and talk.

01 Vocabulary

A Word Definition
Underline the word with the given definition.

1 common at a particular time, in a particular place, or among a particular group of people

   Rumors of a bankruptcy had been prevalent in recent days.

2 a serious disease in which there is too much sugar in your blood

   Most type 2 diabetes is found in adults who are obese.

3 a moral or legal duty to do something

   We have a moral obligation to protect the environment.

4 able to be done or completed

   What the government has suggested is not doable at all.

B Word Use
Write your own sentence using the underlined word in the sentence.

1 I am responsible for the **consequences** of my actions.

   _____

2 Jaggers who are out of shape **huff and puff** during their runs.

   _____

3 Everyone has a right to express their opinions, but it shouldn't **come at the cost of others**!

   _____

4 It didn't even **occur to** me that I'd never see you again.

   _____

02 Presentation

Watch the presentation and answer the questions below.

 Nilofer Merchant talks about how effective walking and talking can be. She talks about the reasons for starting this practice. She also sends a message of encouragement from what she learned by walking and talking.

* Video may not be available depending on the connection to Youtube

A What's the presentation about?

_____
_____

B What's the purpose of this presentation?

_____
_____

C Summarize the story and present it to the class.

_____
_____
_____
_____
_____

03 Presentation (1)

Watch the presentation again and fill in the blanks.

What you're doing, right now, at this very moment, is killing you. More than cars or the Internet or even that little mobile device we keep talking about, the technology you're using the most almost every day is this, your tush. Nowadays people are sitting 9.3 hours a day, which is more than we're sleeping, at 7.7 hours. Sitting is so incredibly (1)_____, we don't even question how much we're doing it, and because everyone else is doing it, it doesn't even occur to us that it's not okay. In that way, sitting has become the (2)_____ of our generation.

Of course there's health consequences to this, scary ones, besides the waist. Things like breast cancer and colon cancer are directly tied to our lack of physical activity, Ten percent in fact, on both of those. Six percent for heart disease, seven percent for type 2 diabetes, which is what my father died of. Now, any of those stats should (3)_____ each of us to get off our duff more, but if you're anything like me, it won't.

What did get me moving was a social (4)_____. Someone invited me to a meeting, but couldn't manage to fit me in to a regular sort of conference room meeting, and said, "I have to walk my dogs tomorrow. Could you come then?" It seemed kind of odd to do, and actually, that first meeting, I remember thinking, "I have to be the one to ask the next question," because I knew I was going to huff and puff during this conversation. And yet, I've taken that idea and made it my own. So instead of going to coffee meetings or fluorescent-lit conference room meetings, I ask people to go on a walking meeting, to the tune of 20 to 30 miles a week. It's changed my life.

But before that, what actually happened was, I used to think about it as, you could take care of your health, or you could take care of (5)_____, and one always came at the cost of the other. So now, several hundred of these walking meetings later, I've learned a few things.

First, there's this amazing thing about actually getting out of the box that leads to out-of-the-box thinking. Whether it's nature or the exercise itself, it certainly works.

And second, and probably the more (6)_____ one, is just about how much each of us can hold problems in (7)_____ when they're really not that way. And if we're going to solve problems and look at the world really differently, whether it's in governance or business or environmental issues, job creation, maybe we can think about how to reframe those problems as having both things be true. Because it was when that happened with this walk-and-talk idea that things became doable and sustainable and viable.

So I started this talk talking about the tush, so I'll end with the (8)_____ line, which is, walk and talk. Walk the talk. You'll be surprised at how fresh air drives fresh thinking, and in the way that you do, you'll bring into your life an entirely new set of ideas.

Thank you.

07 Exercise

A Underline the best word to complete each sentence.

1 The (bottom / under) line is that it's not profitable.

2 Did it (obscure / occur) to you that some people don't care about money?

B Fill in the blanks with the given words.

• prevalent	• convince	• reflective
• lack	• viable	• fluorescent

1 Autism is _____ and 1 in every 500 people are affected.

2 My job is to determine how _____ an option this is.

3 He managed to _____ voters that he was honest.

4 Let's replace ordinary light bulbs with _____ ones.

C Fill in the blanks with the given words.

- come at the cost of
- think out of the box
- is directly tied to
- have an obligation to

1 What we need to do is _____.

2 We all want justice, but that justice should not _____ our humanity.

3 Employers _____ treat all employees equally.

4 The health of our economy _____ how we take care our own health.

Unit 06

Analyzing

 Warm-up

1. A persuasive and successful presentation has enough evidence to get agreement from audience. How do you usually analyze and collect data?

2. How do you show the data you collected: in a graph, chart, or table? Which do you prefer and which is most effective for presentations related to your work?

01 Vocabulary

A Word Definition
Underline the word with the given definition.

1 (of an increase) becoming more and more rapid

   We know that cloud computing is an industry experiencing exponential growth.

2 to gradually get more and more money, possessions, knowledge etc. over a period of time

   Do you know variable annuities can help you accumulate assets for retirement?

3 to be so big that other things are made to seem very small

   The female guest in her high heels seems to dwarf the male host.

4 not willing to forgive or excuse people's faults or wrongdoings

   Marketing is considered a brutal and unforgiving business in Korea.

B Word Use
Write your own sentence using the underlined word in the sentence.

1 Today, I can tell you seven ways your business can **grab** a large market share in Portugal.

   _____

2 I often used to **picture** what it would be like to be a Chief Executive Officer.

   _____

3 He has criticized the corporation's top executives for displaying **sheer** incompetence in managing Don Keith.

   _____

4 The French mountain bike market has been on an **upward** trend since March.

   _____

02 Expression

A Key Expressions

1 if I could draw your attention to the screen
   - If I could draw your attention to the screen, you will see the current British fashion market and how it has been growing over the last decade.
   - If I could draw your attention to the screen, you will see the current U.S. healthcare system and its problems.

2 show exponential growth in
   - This data here shows exponential growth in the number of Internet users in Indonesia.
   - The alternative medicine industry is showing exponential growth in profit.

3 be ranked ... in the ...
   - New Zealand is ranked the fifth most socially advanced country in the world this year.
   - Dustin Johnson is ranked the seventh best golf player in the world.

4 see a continuous increase in
   - Can we see a continuous increase in business?
   - It is not a surprise that Switzerland is seeing a continuous increase in U.S. visitors.

5 at the rate at which we are going
   - We can't continue to turn a profit at the rate at which we're going.
   - At the rate at which we're going, we can continue to grow in the new market.

6 show signs of leveling off
   - Our market share is showing signs of leveling off in the U.S., Germany, and the U.K.
   - The American obesity rate is showing signs of leveling off.

7 hit one's lowest [highest] point
   - You are open to the greatest change when you hit your lowest point.
   - Construction demand for steel is expected to hit its highest point in ten years.

8 turn ... around
   - If you were in charge of Volkswagen, how would you turn things around in Japan?
   - We've hired a new director who we believe will turn around the failing project.

03 Presentation (1)

A What's the presentation about?

_____

_____

B Summarize the story and present it to the class.

_____

_____

_____

_____

C Complete the sentences with the phrases in the box.

> · bunch   · gigantic   · dwarfed   · compares

If I could draw your attention to the screen, you will see what the current mobile market is like and how it (1)_____ with other markets. What are some larger markets we can talk about? We can talk about digital cameras, which (2)_____ game console numbers at 94 million units sold to 26 million. Also in 2008, 135 million MP3 players and 209 million personal computers were sold. None of them compare to the (3)_____ mobile market which saw almost 1 billion units sold.

What this means is that one percent of the mobile phone market share equals 10 millions units. This is indeed a huge market. It's easy to picture if you think big and invest, then you're going to sell 10 million phones with a one-percent market share. And this is exactly what we're going to try to do in 2010, our first full year in the market; we're going to sell a whole (4)_____ of devices by grabbing just one percent of the market share.

04 Presentation (2)

Give a presentation for five minutes using the slide below.

You are going to give a presentation about a strategic analysis of your company, which is a search engine. You will introduce the analyzed data in order to prove that your company is very competitive in the web service industry. Make an introduction using the following slides.

Country Analysis

County	Users(Mn)	Usage Growth (2012~2018)
U.S.	225.00	120.80%
China	177.00	560%
Germany	91.30	82.3%
Brazil	54.15	740%
U.K.	38.15	652.8%
World	1280.00	238%

05 Sample Presentation

Read the script below aloud with proper rhythm and pronunciation.

Good afternoon ladies and gentlemen, thank you for making time to be here. I know you have a tight schedule, so I will try to make this as brief as possible. I'm going to divide this presentation into two categories. A. Is Eagle in the right industry? B. An analysis of the industry.

We here at Eagle have shown exponential growth in recent months and we are now in the top four list of companies providing services in the Web service industry. Let me introduce the results of our analysis on the data that we have accumulated over recent months to prove that our company is indeed very competitive in the Web service industry. If I could draw your attention to the screen, you will notice that we are ranked fourth in the world as far as providing Web services goes. At the rate at which we are going, we will continue to see an upward trend and increased numbers every month. We are showing growth on a daily basis and it seems we are not showing signs of leveling off any time soon.

Presentation Tip

Move Away from the Podium

Get closer to your audience by moving away from or in front of the podium. The podium is a barrier between you and the audience, but the goal of our presentation is to connect with the audience. Removing physical barriers between you and the audience will help you build rapport and make a connection.

06 Mr. Q's Presentation

🎧 **Listen to Mr. Q's presentation and answer the questions below.**

1 Why does Mr. Q call their industry unforgiving?

    ⓐ Prices are always low.   ⓑ There's heavy competition.

    ⓒ Raw materials are expensive.   ⓓ Customers are dwindling.

2 What is the presentation going to show?

    ⓐ Pie charts   ⓑ Survey results

    ⓒ Data analysis   ⓓ Election results

3 According to the speaker, how did they increase their market share?

_____

_____

_____

BUSINESS JOKES

A man was the first to arrive at work one morning. The phone rang and he answered. When the caller asked for some specific information, the man would help if he could. "What's your job there?" the caller asked. The man replied, "I'm the company president." There was a pause. Then the caller said, "I'll call back later. I need to talk to someone who knows something about what's going on."

07 Exercise

A Underline the best word to complete each sentence.

1 We see a (continuous / ambiguous) increase in the global demand for automobiles.

2 Rising gas prices seem to show signs of (revealing / leveling) off.

B Fill in the blanks with the given words.

- exponential
- draw
- accumulated
- grabbing
- dwarfed
- sheer

1 The age of _____ growth in technology could be redoubled with improved battery technology.

2 Wage increases are often _____ by rising commodity prices.

3 It is by the _____ dedication of our employees that we are being recognized as the best cleaning service in the city.

4 We have _____ everything you see in this warehouse in order to have a grand warehouse sale.

C Fill in the blanks with the given words.

- hit their highest point last month
- while Korea tops the list
- grab market share in the coming years
- to turn things around in less than six months

1 The new management team reiterated their commitment _____.

2 U.S. stocks _____, and have since been on a downward spiral.

3 Market analysts doubt that Microsoft's new operating system will _____.

4 The U.S. is ranked thirteenth in public education _____.

Unit 07

Making Comparisons

 Warm-up

1. Comparisons help people to understand similarities and differences more easily. How do you think you can show comparisons effectively?

2. Have you used comparisons in your presentation? Why did you make a comparison? How effective do you think it was?

01 Vocabulary

A Word Definition
Underline the word with the given definition.

1 clearly different or belonging to a different type

When launching a product, you should give it a distinct name to avoid any confusion among potential customers.

2 to reach an agreement in which everyone involved accepts less than what they wanted at first

Lawmakers have been under pressure to compromise on welfare cuts.

3 causing harm or damage

Currently, more than ten cosmetic products, which are considered detrimental to human health, are on the market.

4 having an important effect or influence

It was one of the most significant economic development projects in the last several decades.

B Word Use
Write your own sentence using the underlined word in the sentence.

1 As we all worked a lot last week, **comparatively** little has to be done this week.

_____

2 We have to sell our digital camera division to **make up for** the stock losses.

_____

3 The US housing market has continued to rise at a **steady** pace since January.

_____

4 Analysts have **forecast** India's growth will rise by up to 8 percent for the next five years.

_____

02 Expression

A Key Expressions

1 A is comparable [similar] to B in
- The new logo is comparable to the old one in its design.
- The new Starbucks tumbler is similar to the one from Dunkin' Donuts in size.

2 A and B take up ...% and ...%, respectively
- The smart TV and smartphone markets take up 3% and 10%, respectively.
- The hybrid and electric car markets take up 13% and 20%, respectively.

3 there are a number of similarities between A and B
- There are a number of similarities between the Indian and Pakistani cultures.
- There are a number of similarities between Naver Map and Google Maps.

4 A comparison between A and B reveals
- A comparison between Yamaha and Kawai pianos reveals some interesting facts.
- A comparison between iOS apps and Android apps reveals a growing revenue gap.

5 be based on data comparing
- His research is based on data comparing various customer behaviors in Tokyo.
- My report is based on data comparing the market shares of medical devices in New York.

6 to start off with
- I'd like to start off with some updates on our sales figures.
- I want to start off with a couple of questions.

7 in comparison to [with]
- The Premium Membership will give you greater benefits in comparison to the Standard Membership.
- Oil refinery businesses are much more profitable in comparison with other industries.

8 A is about the same as B
- SecureIt LE is about the same as SecureIt Pro, except for the fact that the latter offers free customer service.
- Surprisingly, your sales figures are about the same as John's.

03 Presentation (1)

A What's the presentation about?

_____
_____

B Summarize the story and present it to the class.

_____
_____
_____
_____

C Complete the sentences with the phrases in the box.

> · compromises   · comparison   · boast   · consistently

What is the MaxioFeather? It's the world's thinnest laptop. When we look at all the ultra-thin laptops out there, the strongest seller is (1)_____ Wiba's Webzin series. A comparison between the MaxioFeather and the Webzin reveals several things. The weight of the Webzin is three pounds which is about the same as most standard laptops. Its cases are about 0.8 to 1.2 inches in thickness and have a wedge shape. The Webzin maker (2)_____ on things like the display in order to get the weight down. The Webzin has an 11- or 12-inch display, most of them 11. Its maker also compromises on the keyboard. Instead of putting in full-size keyboards, they make miniature keyboards.

We think the weight, 3 pounds, is a good target. But we think there's too much compromising to get there. We want a full-size keyboard, and we think we can put even more performance in there. Let's take a look at the MaxioFeather in (3)_____ with the Webzin. The MaxioFeather displays (4)_____ a thickness of only 0.16-0.76 inches, compared to 0.80-1.20 inches for the Webzin.

04 Presentation (2)

Give a presentation for five minutes using the slide below.

You are giving a presentation about a new marketing strategy for your mobile phone products. Based on the data on the following slide, you will identify the market trend and forecast mobile usage in 2018. You need to convince your client to use your marketing strategy.

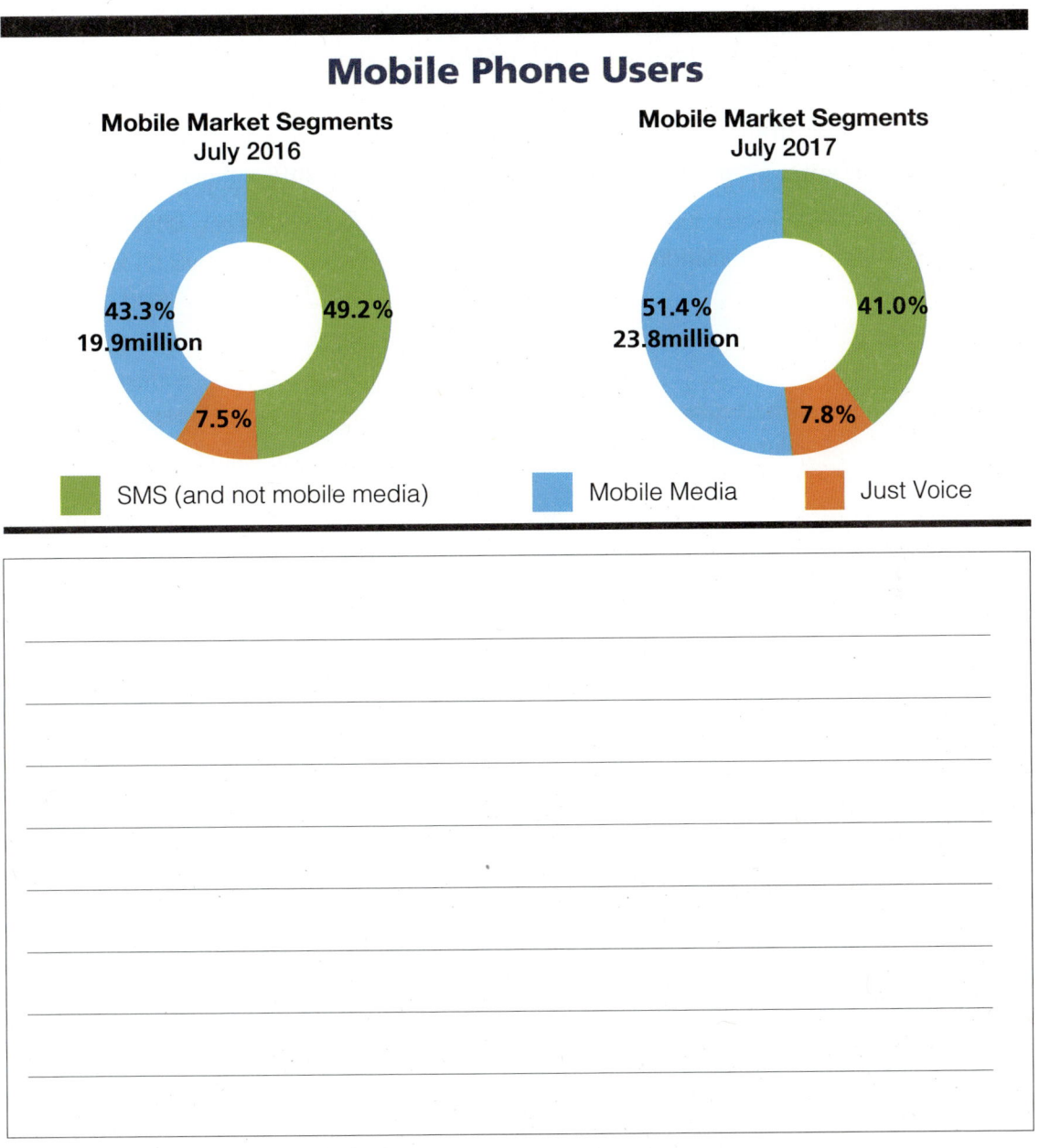

05 Sample Presentation

Read the script below aloud with proper rhythm and pronunciation.

Good afternoon everyone and thank you for joining us today. We will be presenting a new marketing strategy for your mobile phone products. Our presentation is based on data comparing the usage preferences of mobile phone users from 2016 and 2017, and we will show, through these comparisons, why we feel our marketing strategy will benefit you in 2018. As you can see from this slide, there is a significant increase in mobile media activity when comparing 2016 to 2017, while there has been a decrease in SMS usage and only a small increase in voice only usage.

When we consider 2018 in comparison to 2016 and 2017 we can see a distinct upward trend, and in the same way, we can forecast a steady increase in usage for 2018 without compromising in the SMS sector. Our aim is to increase the number of users in all aspects related to your business.

Presentation Tip

Make Good Eye Contact

This sounds very easy, but a surprisingly large number of presenters fail to do it. If you smile and make eye contact, you are building rapport, which helps the audience to connect with you and your subject. It also helps you to feel less nervous, because you are talking to individuals, not to a great mass of unknown people.

06 Mr. Q's Presentation

Listen to Mr. Q's presentation and answer the questions below.

1 Over the past several months, what did they deep a close eye on?

   ⓐ Meeting venues   ⓑ Record stores

   ⓒ Business plans   ⓓ Competitors' strategies

2 What is suggested that they would find if nothing is done?

   ⓐ Failure   ⓑ Rainfall

   ⓒ New markets   ⓓ New competitors

3 What does the speaker recommend that they do?

   _____

   _____

   _____

BUSINESS JOKES

An elderly gentleman checked into a New York hotel. The clerk mentioned the phone service the establishment made available for calling guests who wished to rise at an early hour. "No need for that, young man," snapped the old timer. "I always wake up at five A.M. sharp without an alarm clock." "Very good, sir," the clerk replied, then asked, "Would you mind calling me at six?"

07 Exercise

A Underline the best word to complete each sentence.

1 There has been a (steady / stiff) increase in burglaries this year in Abilene.
2 There are a number of (simulation / similarities) between our premium and standard services.

B Fill in the blanks with the given words.

- distinct
- comparison
- significant
- respectively
- detrimental
- forecasts

1 A recent survey shows that public feelings and business owners' opinions on the tax increase are _____ from one another.

2 We will soon be able to see some _____ effects caused by climate change.

3 Dick's Sporting Goods Inc. announced on Tuesday it _____ $10 billion in sales by 2020.

4 A major UN report shows a _____ change for the better in Ebola cases in West Africa.

C Fill in the blanks with the given words.

- in comparison with those of China.
- about the same as our competitor's
- this research is based on data
- when comparing the Greek economy

1 Unfortunately, our new model is _____.

2 Russia's strategic plans for gas pipelines are much more advanced _____ _____.

3 There are some similarities _____ to the Italian economy.

4 _____ comparing various business environments across North America.

Unit 08

Making Contrasts

 Warm-up

1 Contrast is one of the best techniques for creating an immediate and remarkable impact. How do you think you can use this technique for your presentation? If you already have, share it with the class.

2 Let's suppose that you've just developed a new product. Which is a more effective contrast for making a strong impression: with a competitor's new product or with a former model of your own product?

01 Vocabulary

A Word Definition

Underline the word with the given definition.

1 someone who copies other people's clothes, behaviour, work etc.

   A number of global companies are waging war on Chinese copycats.

2 minor and not important; not central

   There was a marginal drop in the U.S. unemployment rate in January, which briefly boosted stock markets.

3 an inclination towards a particular characteristic or type of behaviour

   Stock prices show a tendency to increase over time.

4 liable to change rapidly and unpredictably, especially for the worse

   Analysts expect grain prices to remain volatile as the demand for wheat fluctuates.

B Word Use

Write your own sentence using the underlined word in the sentence.

1 It seems that China has almost **caught up with** South Korea's electronics capabilities.

   _____

2 You should not **rest on your laurels,** but keep striving in this rapidly-changing world.

   _____

3 I want all of you to **go all out** in our quest to reclaim the market.

   _____

4 Android has become the most popular **end-user** operating system, with one billion users, worldwide.

   _____

62 BUSINESS INTERACTION *Presentation*

02 Expression

A Key Expressions

1 A differs from B in a number of important ways
- This year's budget differs from the previous one in a number of important ways.
- The federal education system differs from the states' in a number of important ways.

2 A and B are different in several ways
- Software analysts and software business analysts are different in several ways.
- Social democrats and liberal democrats are different in several ways.

3 A varies from B in the fact that
- My plans vary from Greg's in the fact that mine are all about priorities.
- Gas prices vary from city to city in the fact that each city has different factors, like taxes.

4 There are several differences between A and B
- There are several differences between your official plan and the contingency plan.
- What should we do so that there can be more than minor differences between the old model and the new one?

5 on the other hand
- Living in a cold climate is painful for some people. On the other hand, we enjoy many fun winter activities, such as skiing and snowboarding.
- We often have to work late. On the other hand, we certainly have the best salaries in the industry.

6 A is [are] twice as ... as B
- The new DeskPro is almost twice as powerful as the previous model.
- The new door lock is twice as safe as the old one.

7 in contrast to
- In contrast to stocks, investments in bonds increase gradually.
- The foreign investment system in China is vey insular, in contrast to those in most European countries.

8 As a matter of fact
- As a matter of fact, he helped us implement the maintenance procedure.
- As a matter of fact, it is quite a distance to travel, so I will refer you to our nearest repair center.

03 Presentation (1)

A What's the presentation about?

_____

_____

B Summarize the story and present it to the class.

_____

_____

_____

_____

C Complete the sentences with the phrases in the box.

> • catch up   • exceptional   • achievement   • improvements

We've gotten off to an (1)_____ first year and we plan to build on that. What about 2020? Everybody's got a tablet PC. Is 2020 going to be the year of the copycats?

Well, I think if we do nothing, we'll be fine, because most of these tablets still need to (2)_____ with the first Maxreen. But we haven't been resting on our laurels because, in less than a year, we're going to introduce the Maxreen 2, the second generation of the Maxreen.

Maxreen 2 differs from the Maxreen in several ways. It is an all-new design. These are not just marginal (3)_____. It is a completely new product. We've really gone all out on the graphics performance, with graphics up to seven times faster. We don't want to give up any of the legendary battery life. So, the Maxreen 2 is really quite an (4)_____ and is going to give us something that's up to twice as much as what you might see from a PC.

04 Presentation (2)

Give a presentation for five minutes using the slide below.

You are giving a presentation about innovative marketing strategies. Through contrast, report on the competitiveness of your company (Yahoo). At the same time, mention relevent customer data.

Top Competitors

Brand	Visitors	Time spent
Yahoo	99.135	3:08:06
Microsoft	93.500	0:45:51
MSN	90.602	1:43:37
Google	76.901	0:39:45
AOL	74.460	6:22:20
eBay	52.098	1:58:14
Amazon	36.086	0:21:05
Weather Channel	30.305	0:27:36

05 Sample Presentation

Read the script below aloud with proper rhythm and pronunciation.

> The topic of our presentation today is innovative marketing strategies. As the market leader in our industry, we are confident in the strong competitiveness of our company. Despite several differences between us and our competitors, and the fact that our platform varies from theirs, the tendency of end users is to go with brand-name companies.
>
> As a matter of fact, studies have shown that end users, or "Joe Public", would rather use a well-recognized brand name than a "no-name" brand, even if the "no-name" brand is superior in quality. It's due to this fact that we remain at the top of the board. Customer tendencies are nearly impossible to predict in today's volatile market and, in this respect, we need to maintain our leading position and continue to strive to provide exceptional service to our customers.

Presentation Tip

Remember the 10-20-30 Rule for Slideshows

Slideshows should contain no more than 10 slides, last no more than 20 minutes, and use a font size of no less than 30 point. This last is particularly important as it stops you trying to put too much information on any one slide. As a general rule, slides should be the sideshow to you, the presenter.

06 Mr. Q's Presentation

🎧 **Listen to Mr. Q's presentation and answer the questions below.**

1 What is most likely the subject of the presentation?

ⓐ Conducting surveys   ⓑ Negotiating with clients

ⓒ Investing in websites   ⓓ Attracting customers

2 What company does the speaker most likely represent?

ⓐ Facebook   ⓑ Yahoo

ⓒ Google   ⓓ Sprint

3 What do you think the speaker's main point is?

_____

_____

_____

BUSINESS JOKES

Two friends were talking together over a cup of coffee. They started talking about business and one of them said, "It seems like all I do at the office is fight with Jack. I've been so down lately. I've lost 15 pounds." "Why don't you just leave the job then?" asked the friend. "Oh! Not yet. I'd like to lose at least another 10 pounds first!"

UNIT 08 Making Contrasts

07 Exercise

A Underline the best word to complete each sentence.

1 Despite unstable oil prices, most airline companies in the US reported (marginal / marital) increases profit last year.

2 The struggling world economy stands in (contract / contrast) to the health of U.S. companies.

B Fill in the blanks with the given words.

- volatile
- previous
- end users
- copycat
- implement
- tendency

1 Social networking services like Facebook constantly stimulate our _____ to mimic people in our social circles.

2 The catchphrase of our new anti-piracy campaign is "stop being a _____ and be original!"

3 We should hold more training sessions to teach our _____ on how to get more out of our products.

4 U.S. housing rose slightly in March, but home trading was still _____.

C Fill in the blanks with the given words.

- as a matter of fact
- in a number of important ways
- more than twice as
- on the other hand

1 The Consumer Price Index differs from the Wholesale Price Index _____ _____.

2 Living in the city is convenient. _____ rural life is a lot less stressful.

3 These days the costs of application software are _____ expensive as those of hardware.

4 _____ G-mart has never been considered the best grocery chain in the US.

Unit 09

Emphasizing

 Warm-up

1. If you want to stress/emphasize some points in your presentation, who do you think it can be done effectively?
2. Which do you think is more effective: to raise your voice, use gestures, or make handouts/slides? Give some reasons for your preference.

01 Vocabulary

A Word Definition

Underline the word with the given definition.

1 serving as a means of pursuing an aim

   Former Ohio Congressman, George Russell, was **instrumental** in securing investors.

2 something that shows what something else is like, or that is a sign of a particular situation

   A low debt-to-equity ratio is a **reflection** of a company's financial strength.

3 to teach someone to think, behave, or feel in a particular way over a period of time

   Here are the eleven strategies to **instill** an entrepreneurial spirit in your child.

4 very big, fast, powerful, etc.

   Bellway International has announced **tremendous** growth for the third consecutive year.

B Word Use

Write your own sentence using the underlined word in the sentence.

1 The unprecedented drought is now **driving** a national interest in desalination.

   _____

2 Wikileaks files have revealed the **inner workings** of the secretive government.

   _____

3 Chinese electronics makers are currently striving for **brand recognition** in the European market.

   _____

4 I would like to talk about seven simple ways to ensure **repeat business.**

   _____

02 Expression

A Key Expressions

1 I'd like to stress [highlight/emphasize]
- I'd like to stress the importance of social media skills.
- I'd like to stress the importance of recycling.

2 it is critical that
- It is critical that you nail your niche market.
- It is critical that the CFO be an active participant in all business decisions.

3 I'd like to focus your attention on
- I'd like to focus your attention on Denver's housing problem.
- I'd like to focus your attention on building an economy that works for the future.

4 What I'd like to point out is that
- What I'd like to point out is that cultural diversity can mean lots of things to lots of people.
- What I'd like to point out is that humans are more rational and autonomous than animals.

5 What is essential to us is
- What is essential to us is how much work can be accomplished on the weekends.
- What is essential to us is to start investing.

6 put the spotlight on
- West Kirby filmmakers put the spotlight on Hilbre Island.
- Singapore's success puts a global spotlight on its corporate leaders.

7 cannot stress it enough
- Those in the business of patrolling our highways cannot stress the importance of seat belts enough.
- I cannot stress it enough. It's up to us.

8 cannot ignore that
- We cannot ignore that we do business to make a profit.
- We cannot ignore that we have made remarkable progress.

03 Presentation (1)

A What's the presentation about?

_____

_____

B Summarize the story and present it to the class.

_____

_____

_____

_____

C Complete the sentences with the phrases in the box.

> • initiated   • attention   • spotlight   • stress

Good morning, everyone. As you know, Pyeongchang has been honored with the right to host the Winter Olympic Games in 2018. It is a very grand achievement for the entire country. What I' like to focus your (1)_____ on today is the "Drive the Dream" project which was (2)_____ by the South Korean government several years ago. This program has been instrumental in not only bringing the Olympics to Pyeongchang but also driving national interest in winter sports in general. At the end of this talk, I will put the (3)_____ on the program's benefits including the building of training facilities, the funding of training programs, and the promotion of winter sports.

However, there has been talk that the program is just a waste of public money. Let me point out that thanks to this program, more than 1,500 youths have registered for winter sports programs in the last five years. It is absolutely critical that we continue this program not only to keep the Olympic spirit alive but also for the future of young people in this country. They deserve the opportunity to pursue their dreams. I cannot (4)_____ it enough. Please keep the program alive. For our youths. For our future.

04 Presentation (2)

Give a presentation for five minutes using the slide below.

You are giving a presentation in order to report on the international operations of Starcoffee. With the following slide, you should emphasize the success factors with some examples based on your experience in coffee shops.

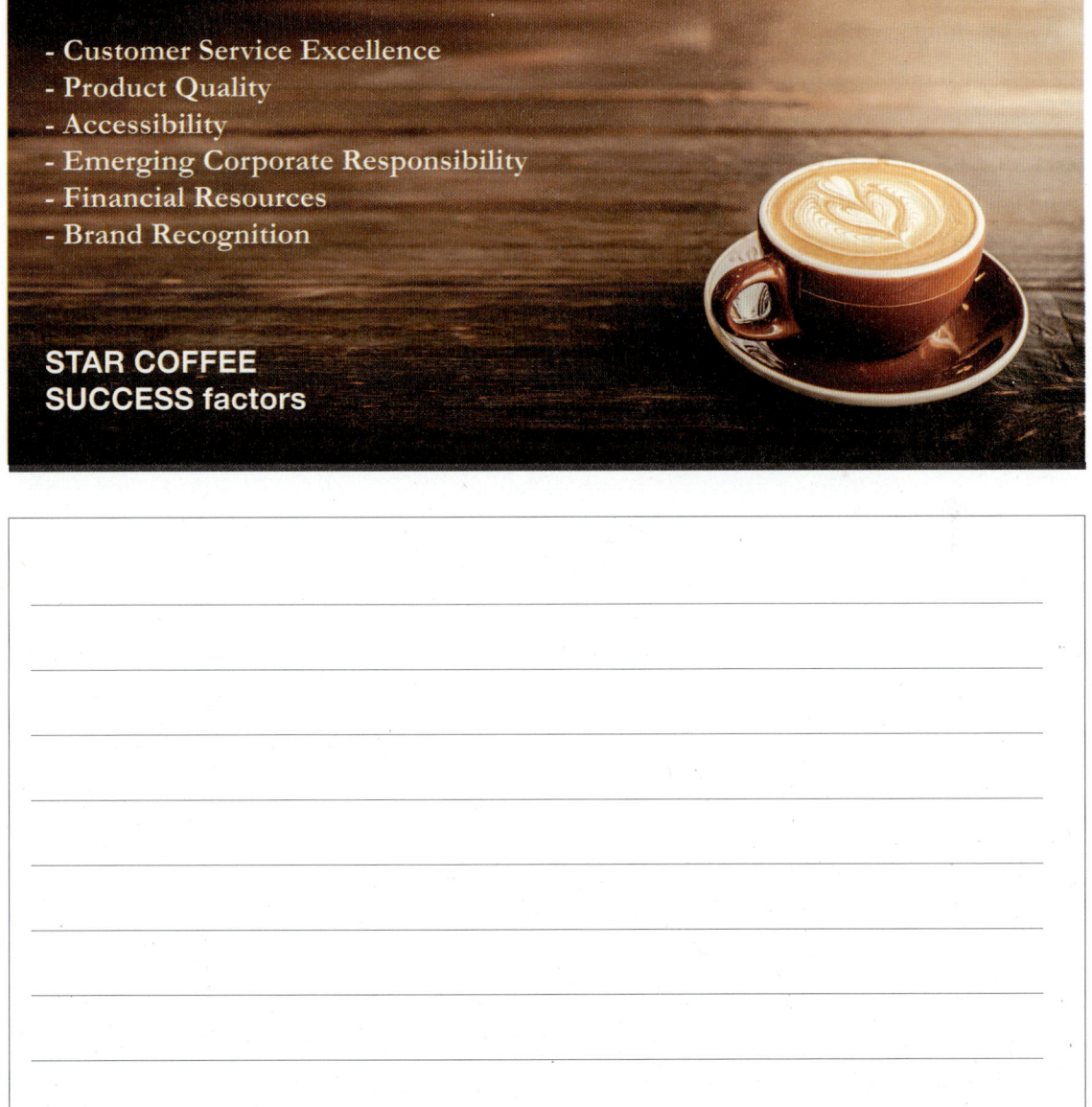

- Customer Service Excellence
- Product Quality
- Accessibility
- Emerging Corporate Responsibility
- Financial Resources
- Brand Recognition

STAR COFFEE SUCCESS factors

05 Sample Presentation

Read the script below aloud with proper rhythm and pronunciation.

Good day everybody and thank you for joining me. We have come together to report on the international operations of Star Coffee. It is essential that we understand the inner workings of Star Coffee in order to get a true reflection of what they offer. I would like to focus our attention on three major points: customer service, product quality, and brand recognition. I would also like to emphasize the importance of accessibility, emerging corporate responsibilities, and financial recourses.

What I would like to point out at this moment is that the executive members of the group have a combined business-related experience of over 55 years in the coffee industry. What is essential to us is how to convey this to the shareholders in order to instill a vote of confidence in them.

As I'm sure you are aware, the coffee industry is massive and there is a tremendous amount of competition out there. This is where Star Coffee needs to turn buying a cup of coffee into a coffee experience to secure repeat business from its customers.

Presentation Tip

Focus on Your Audience's Needs

Your presentation needs to be built around what your audience is going to get out of the presentation. As you prepare the presentation, you always need to bear in mind what the audience needs and wants to know, not what you can tell them. While you're giving the presentation, you also need to remain focused on your audience's response, and react to that.

06 Mr. Q's Presentation

🎧 **Listen to Mr. Q's presentation and answer the questions below.**

1 Which of the following companies is the speaker talking about?

   ⓐ Starbucks   ⓑ Star Coffee

   ⓒ McDonald's   ⓓ Red Orange

2 What is the reason the company in question has become a leader in the industry?

   ⓐ A wide range of products   ⓑ Investments in social media

   ⓒ Superb customer service   ⓓ TV advertisements

3 What else does the speaker emphasize during his presentation?

   _____

   _____

   _____

BUSINESS JOKES

A fresh graduate from a prestigious business school was hired by the supermarket that I manage. When he reported to the first day of work, I handed him a broom and dustpan and told him to sweep up the store. "But I'm a college grad!" he whined. "Oh I'm sorry," I replied. "give me the broom and I'll show you how to do it!"

07 Exercise

A Underline the best word to complete each sentence.

1 It is (absurd / critical) that we work together to the end.

2 What I'd like to (rule / point) out is that most of its executive members are from large mining companies.

B Fill in the blanks with the given words.

- instill
- ignore
- instrumental
- strives
- drives
- tremendous

1 Japanese universities always try to _____ a global mindset in their students.

2 What _____ the CEO to work as hard as he does?

3 We have made a _____ effort to focus on privacy issues.

4 She will be _____ in developing and implementing new financial strategies.

C Fill in the blanks with the given words.

- will put the spotlight on
- are a reflection of
- stress the importance of
- is essential to us is

1 I would like to _____ early childhood education.

2 High sales _____ a company's economic health.

3 What _____ how long we can maintain our financial stability.

4 Today's meeting _____ the need to boost the availability of skills training in Brantford.

Actual Case 2

Unit 10

The Jobs We'll Lose to Machines — and the Ones We Won't

Anthony Goldbloom

Machine learning isn't just for simple tasks like assessing credit risk and sorting mail anymore-today, it's capable of far more complex applications, like grading essays and diagnosing diseases. With these advances comes an uneasy question: Will a robot do your job in the future?

01 Vocabulary

A Word Definition
Underline the word with the given definition.

1 to make a judgment about a person or situation after thinking carefully about it

   It's difficult to **assess** the effects of these changes.

2 to start using computers and machines to do a job, rather than people

   We wanted to use computers to **automate** the process.

3 to be more successful than someone or something else

   Korean companies are known for striving to **outperform** their competitors.

4 consisting of things or people that are very different and not related to each other

   The total economic picture is the sum of many **disparate** parts.

B Word Use
Write your own sentence using the underlined word in the sentence.

1 They **brought together** an immense amount of scattered data.

   _____

2 This test is sometimes used to **diagnose** and monitor asthma.

   _____

3 This area suffers to some **extent** from flooding.

   _____

4 The company has been in **litigation** with its previous auditors for a full year.

   _____

02 Presentation

Watch the presentation and answer the questions below.

Anthony Goldbloom introduces a technology called machine learning, which he suggests to be the most powerful branch of a certain technology. He suggests that the development of machine learning will impact the future labor force and recommends certain types of jobs to adapt to this shift.

*Video may not be available depending on the connection to Youtube

A What's the presentation about?

_____
_____

B What's the purpose of this presentation?

_____
_____

C Summarize the story and present it to the class.

_____
_____
_____
_____
_____

03 Transcript

Give a presentation for five minutes using the slide below.

So this is my niece. Her name is Yahli. She is nine months old. Her mum is a doctor, and her dad is a lawyer. By the time Yahli goes to college, the jobs her parents do are going to look (1)_____ different.

In 2013, researchers at Oxford University did a study on the future of work. They concluded that almost one in every two jobs have a high risk of being automated by machines. Machine learning is the technology that's responsible for most of this (2)_____. It's the most powerful branch of artificial intelligence. It allows machines to learn from data and (3)_____ some of the things that humans can do. My company, Kaggle, operates on the cutting edge of machine learning. We bring together hundreds of thousands of experts to solve important problems for industry and academia. This gives us a unique perspective on what machines can do, what they can't do, and what jobs they might automate or threaten.

Machine learning started making its way into industry in the early '90s. It started with relatively simple tasks. It started with things like assessing credit risk from loan applications, sorting the mail by reading handwritten characters from zip codes. Over the past few years, we have made dramatic (4)_____. Machine learning is now capable of far, far more complex tasks. In 2012, Kaggle challenged its community to build an algorithm that could grade high-school essays. The winning algorithms were able to match the grades given by human teachers. Last year, we issued an even more difficult challenge. Can you take images of the eye and diagnose an eye disease called diabetic retinopathy? Again, the winning algorithms were able to match the diagnoses given by human ophthalmologists.

Now, given the right data, machines are going to (5)_____ humans at tasks like this. A teacher might read 10,000 essays over a 40-year career. An ophthalmologist might see 50,000 eyes. A machine can read millions of essays or see millions of eyes within minutes. We have no chance of competing against machines on frequent, high-volume tasks.

But there are things we can do that machines can't do. Where machines have made very little progress is in tackling novel situations. They can't handle things they haven't seen many times before. The fundamental limitations of machine learning is that it needs to learn from large volumes of past data. Now, humans don't. We have the ability to connect seemingly (6)_____ threads to solve problems we've never seen before.

Percy Spencer was a physicist working on radar during World War II, when he noticed the magnetron was melting his chocolate bar. He was able to connect his understanding of electromagnetic radiation with his knowledge of cooking in order to invent – any guesses? - the microwave oven.

Now, this is a particularly remarkable example of creativity. But this sort of cross-pollination happens for each of us in small ways thousands of times per day. Machines cannot compete with us when it comes to tackling novel situations, and this puts a fundamental limit on the human tasks that machines will automate.

So what does this mean for the future of work? The future state of any single job lies in the answer to a single question: To what extent is that job (7)_____ to frequent, high-volume tasks, and to what extent does it involve tackling novel situations? On frequent, high-volume tasks, machines are getting smarter and smarter. Today they grade essays. They diagnose certain diseases. Over coming years, they're going to conduct our audits, and they're going to read boilerplate from legal contracts. Accountants and lawyers are still needed. They're going to be needed for complex tax structuring, for pathbreaking litigation. But machines will (8)_____ their ranks and make these jobs harder to come by.

Now, as mentioned, machines are not making progress on novel situations. The copy behind a marketing campaign needs to grab consumers' attention. It has to stand out from the crowd. Business strategy means finding gaps in the market, things that nobody else is doing. It will be humans that are creating the copy behind our marketing campaigns, and it will be humans that are developing our business strategy.

So Yahli, whatever you decide to do, let every day bring you a new challenge. If it does, then you will stay ahead of the machines.

Thank you.

07 Exercise

A Underline the best word to complete each sentence.

1 This (artificial / articulate) rose is quite lifelike.

2 The (frequent / precarious) name changes have confused citiaens even more.

B Fill in the blanks with the given words.

- algorithm
- mimic
- breakthrough
- disparate
- diagnose
- outperform

1 Parrots are known to _____ people and noises they hear.

2 These methods are used to _____ heart attacks in adults.

3 We still have very _____ points of view.

4 The discovery was perceived as a major _____.

C Fill in the blanks with the given words.

- have no chance of
- have a higher risk of
- the extent of the damage
- bring people together

1 Women older than age 35 _____ miscarriage than younger women.

2 As governor, I would like to _____.

3 If we don't do that, we _____ winning.

4 We were shocked at _____ to my car.

Unit 11

Introducing Visuals

 Warm-up

1. Have you ever seen a presentation by Steve Jobs? What's your opinion of his slides? What do think he wants to say with his visual aids? Why do you think they are effective?

2. Have you ever used any visual aids? What did you use them for? Where they effective? Share your experience with the class.

01 Vocabulary

A Word Definition
Underline the word with the given definition.

1 to describe something in a way that makes it seem less important or serious than it really is

If you say that things can operate on a small budget, you must be understating the situation.

2 to move back and away from something, especially because you are frightened

Jacqueline shrank in fear after she was reprimanded by her boss.

3 to formally approve a proposal, amendment, etc, especially by voting

The European Union has adopted a great number of measures to improve its fiscal governance.

4 to make something using a special skill, especially with your hands

These bracelets were crafted by native Australians.

B Word Use
Write your own sentence using the underlined word in the sentence.

1 **Fast forward** to today, and she is selling about 200 bags a day on her website.

_____

2 It might be time to take strong action against anyone who **spills** corporate secrets.

_____

3 The UAE's old library has **stood** the test of time.

_____

4 Utah center Jacob Poeltl will **bypass** the NBA draft and return for his sophomore year.

_____

02 Expression

A Key Expressions

1 draw your attention to
  - Let me begin by drawing your attention to our first slide.
  - I'd like to draw your attention to this fact.

2 The first slide demonstrates
  - The first slide demonstrates the economic problems the U.S. faces.
  - The first slide demonstrates how to prevent domestic violence.

3 be marked in white
  - Our existing customers' names are marked in white.
  - Important questions are marked in red.

4 To illustrate [illuminate] this
  - To illustrate this, simply take a look at this screen.
  - To illuminate this, we need a discussion about it as soon as possible.

5 let's have a closer look at
  - Let's have a closer look at the crime scene.
  - Let's have a closer look at the survey results.

6 I have put ... on a handout
  - I have put the new price list on a handout.
  - I have put all the important facts on a handout.

7 take one and pass them on
  - You will not need to take notes as I have some handouts, so please take one and pass them on.
  - Please don't forget to take one and pass them on.

8 in the bottom [upper] left-[right]-hand corner
  - You will find the logo in the bottom right hand corner.
  - Leave your phone in the upper left hand corner.

03 Presentation (1)

A What's the presentation about?

_____

_____

B Summarize the story and present it to the class.

_____

_____

_____

_____

C Complete the sentences with the phrases in the box.

> · contracts   · demonstrates   · understates   · permanent

The first slide, which is from the year 1980, shows the Arctic ice cap. As you can see, it is roughly the size of Brazil. Let me draw your attention to the next slide which (1)_____ a what's happened over the last 27 years. The (2)_____ ice is marked in bright white. It expands in the winter, and (3)_____ in the summer. This permanent ice which looks like it's spilling out like thick blood has shrunk by nearly half within the last 27 years. But this actually (4)_____ the seriousness of the problem because it doesn't show the actual thickness of the ice. The Arctic ice pack is, in a sense, the beating heart of the global climate system. The more it shrinks the more danger the earth is in.

04 Presentation (2)

Give a presentation for five minutes using the slide below.

Your company just created a new beer and you are giving a presentation about sales to future customers. You are going to highlight a special way of making the new beer using visuals. Using the slide, make the audience aware of differences between the old beers and the new with various qualities such as color, froth, flavor, and so on.

You Have Your ALES & You Have Your LAGERS

UNIT 11 Introducing Visuals

05 Sample Presentation

Read the script below aloud with proper rhythm and pronunciation.

Good morning and welcome to our existing customers, but it is also nice to see so many new faces in the audience. A warm welcome to all of you too. I hope that after this presentation, we can add you to our list of future customers. You will not need to take notes as I have some handouts, so please take one and pass them on.

Let me begin by drawing your attention to our first slide and allow me to highlight the new method we have adopted in crafting our beers. To illustrate this, let' have a closer look at the differences between ales and lagers. Although the method of making beer has stood the test of time, we are confident that this new approach to making beer will be of great interest to you.

Presentation Tip

Don't Read

This one is a no brainer, but somehow PowerPoint makes people think they can get away with it. If you don't know your speech without cues, that doesn't just make you more distracting. It shows you don't really understand your message, a huge blow to any confidence the audience has in you.

06 Mr. Q's Presentation

🎧 **Listen to Mr. Q's presentation and answer the questions below.**

1 What is the topic of the presentation?

　ⓐ A new method of brewing beer　　ⓑ Making hamburger buns at home

　ⓒ How to cook hot dogs　　ⓓ New ways to drink coffee

2 What did Mr. Q most likely give each audience member before the presentation?

　ⓐ A cup of coffee　　ⓑ A handout

　ⓒ A notebook　　ⓓ A business card

3 What does the speaker want to discuss during the taste test?

_____

_____

_____

| BUSINESS JOKES | Faced with hard times, the company offered a bonus of $100.00 to any employee who could come up with a plan to save money. The bonus went to a young man in accounting who suggested limiting future bonuses to $10.00. |

07 Exercise

A Underline the best word to complete each sentence.

1 Let's have a (farther / closer) look at the case.

2 The first slide (demonstrates / demonize) worldwide interest in global warming.

B Fill in the blanks with the given words.

| • understate | • stood | • illuminate |
| • adopt | • craft | • spilled |

1 Gold has always _____ the test of time.

2 It is important that we do not _____ this issue.

3 $37 billion worth of oil has been _____ due to a pipeline accident.

4 The NHRC chairman is asking corporations to _____ a unified approach to social media.

C Fill in the blanks with the given words.

- marked in white
- put an updated contract list
- to illustrate this
- on the bottom right hand corner

1 You can see the page number _____.

2 Non-smokers are _____ on the list.

3 _____, I prepared special charts for you.

4 I have _____ on a handout.

Unit 12

Describing a Bar Graph

 Warm-up

1. What kinds of visuals do you usually use to describe information in your presentation? Share the purpose and effect with the class.

2. Have you ever used bar graphs in a presentation? Was it as effective as you had planned? What do you like about using bar graphs?

01 Vocabulary

A Word Definition
Underline the word with the given definition.

1 the respect and admiration that someone or something gets because of their success or important position in society

   His position at Harvard Medical School now has more prestige than ever.

2 to improve something

   JM Media has decided to enhance security with the JSON firewall.

3 to describe something or someone in writing or speech, or to show them in a painting, picture etc.

   James Wong's paintings mostly depict his early life in Beijing.

4 to do something very well, or much better than most people

   He has excelled in all aspects of acting.

B Word Use
Write your own sentence using the underlined word in the sentence.

1 Markets work and economies are guided **by means of** an invisible hand.

_____

2 A recent study shows that too much jogging may shorten your **life span**.

_____

3 Home buyers seem to have the **upper hand** in this market.

_____

4 It was **apparent** from her face that she was really upset.

_____

02 Expression

A Key Expressions

1 <u>This bar graph deals with</u>
- This bar graph deals with the performance of the MSCI China Group over the past year.
- This bar graph deals with the top ten recorded floods with the largest economic losses.

2 <u>be illustrated in this bar graph</u>
- The global problem of poverty is illustrated in this bar graph.
- This quarter's sales are illustrated in this bar graph.

3 <u>different colors have been used to indicate</u>
- You can see that different colors have been used to indicate the years.
- You can see that different colors have been used to indicate the results.

4 <u>by using the graph as a tool of comparison</u>
- By using the graph as a tool of comparison, we can visually see the difference.
- By using the graph as a tool of comparison, we can show qualitative parameters.

5 <u>Overall, it can be seen that</u>
- Overall, it can be seen that the U.S. dollar will stay on track for 2020.
- Overall, it can be seen that economic factors can have a significant influence on culture and society.

6 <u>there was a steady decrease [increase] in</u>
- There was a steady decrease in mobile traffic from Google.
- There was a steady increase in meat imports.

7 <u>far outweigh</u>
- My love of Cambridge far outweighs my dislike for the local cuisine.
- The benefits far outweigh the risks.

8 <u>fall behind</u>
- We are falling behind the UK in pension reform.
- Poor children fall behind in literacy.

03 Presentation (1)

A What's the presentation about?

_____

_____

B Summarize the story and present it to the class.

_____

_____

_____

_____

C Complete the sentences with the phrases in the box.

- simply   · deals   · scrutiny   · compared

Hello. My name is Josh Candrace and I'm here to talk about our state's education budget. This bar graph here (1)_____ with the 2010 education budget of the state of California (2)_____ to the money spent by big corporations Microsoft and Google in the same year. A huge difference is illustrated in this graph. We can easily see what kind of investments Microsoft and Google are making but where is all the public money going? Where is it being spent? There needs to be more (3)_____ on this. Overall, it can be seen that there's a problem with the allocation of the California state budget. You don't need to be a brain surgeon to figure that out. (4)_____ put, we need better allocation and management of our public money.

BUSINESS INTERACTION *Presentation*

04 Presentation (2)

Give a presentation for five minutes using the slide below.

You are going to explain one of the ways that Blue Tech can beat FruitTronix through the bar graph shown below. Select a difference between the two companies and suggest at least one strategy to take advantage of that difference.

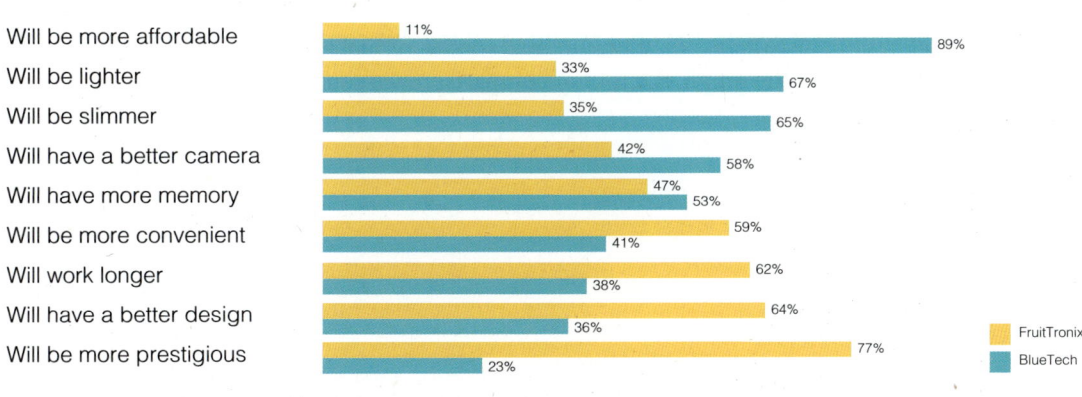

How can BlueTech beat FruitTronix?
Customer expectations of next BlueTech & FruitTronix smartphones.

	FruitTronix	BlueTech
Will be more affordable	11%	89%
Will be lighter	33%	67%
Will be slimmer	35%	65%
Will have a better camera	42%	58%
Will have more memory	47%	53%
Will be more convenient	59%	41%
Will work longer	62%	38%
Will have a better design	64%	36%
Will be more prestigious	77%	23%

05 Sample Presentation

Read the script below aloud with proper rhythm and pronunciation.

> Today we will discuss strategies on how BlueTech can beat FruitTronix and we will do this by means of a bar graph. You can see that different colors have been used to illustrate the two companies.
>
> Let's ask two fundamental questions. What similarities are there and what trends can we see? According to the graph, we can see that BlueTech customer satisfaction far outweighs FruitTronix in many aspects. We should, however, concentrate on the areas where BlueTech is falling behind according to the graph, and these are convenience, life span, design and prestige.
>
> I feel if we focus our attention on these four aspects, we can devise a plan that would further enhance our position and give us the upper hand in taking this company forward and producing winning results. By using the graph as a tool of comparison, we can easily identify problem areas that need to be addressed.

Presentation Tip

Be Entertaining

Speeches should be entertaining and informative. I'm not saying you should act like a dancing monkey when giving a serious presentation. But unlike an e-mail or article, people expect some appeal to their emotions. Simply reciting dry facts without any passion or humor will make people less likely to pay attention.

06 Mr. Q's Presentation

Listen to Mr. Q's presentation and answer the questions below.

1 What are being compared in the bar graph?

   ⓐ Two countries   ⓑ Two people

   ⓒ Two companies   ⓓ Two products

2 What else can be seen in the graph?

   ⓐ Customer confidence levels   ⓑ Sales goals

   ⓒ Marketing strategies   ⓓ Product designs

3 What is illustrated in the speaker's next graph?

   _____

   _____

   _____

BUSINESS JOKES

I waited for a very long time for my number to be called at the Department of Motor Vehicles to renew my driver's license. As I approached the window, the clerk asked how she could help me. I replied, "I need to get a haircut, can you save me my spot?" She said, "Why didn't you get a haircut before you came here?" I replied, "I didn't need one before I got here!"

07 Exercise

A Underline the best word to complete each sentence.

1 GreenPower (excelled / expelled) in the solar energy market last year.

2 Innovation is (falling / failing) behind in parts of the developing world.

B Fill in the blanks with the given words.

• continuous	• prestige	• enhance
• apparent	• depict	• apply

1 Foreign investors are expected to _____ market efficiency in Saudi Arabia.

2 The movie will _____ how the company failed in the end.

3 Many professors at Seoul National University come from backgrounds of _____ and privilege.

4 It is _____ that we will lose money for the second year straight.

C Fill in the blanks with the given words.

- deals with Citigroup's revenue
- far outweigh the costs
- illustrated in this bar graph
- it can be seen that

1 All test results will be_____.

2 This bar graph _____ and net income.

3 Overall, _____ mental health is based on a certain degree of tension.

4 The benefits will _____ in the long run.

Unit 13

Describing a Line Graph

 Warm-up

1. When you use a line graph for your presentation, it helps clearly present the increase and decrease of figures. What other kinds of advantages does it have?

2. What kinds of data do you use a line graph for? Share your experience using them in your presentation.

01 Vocabulary

A Word Definition
Underline the word with the given definition.

1 simple and easy to understand

The line graph for the sugar-free beverages is straightforward to understand.

2 difficult to understand

The relevant data are too obscure to draw any meaningful conclusions.

3 making you feel slightly confused, embarrassed, or worried

The initial sales results were disconcerting when reviewed our overseas business expansion.

4 the amount of business done during a particular period

Since its start in March, Walter's Department Store has recorded a massive $3 billion turnover.

B Word Use
Write your own sentence using the underlined word in the sentence.

1 The stock market crash of 1929 **led to** the Great Depression.

_____

2 A larger proportion of experienced workers appears to be a **contributing factor** for a much lower defect rate than our competitors.

_____

3 The illustration on page 7 is the **depiction** of the outstanding performance of our marketing department.

_____

4 We had to cancel the funding to the local university because a **budget shortfall** was expected.

_____

02 Expression

A Key Expressions

1 illustrate the trend of
- The first graph illustrates the upward trend of smartphone dependence.
- This graph illustrates the downward trend of GDP per capita in Greece for the past five years.

2 based on the following line graph
- We can see higher sales in our new cosmetic lines based on the following line graph.
- The frequency of industrial accidents this year is much lower than last year's based on the following line graph.

3 fluctuate in some way
- Wars always cause the prices of durable goods to fluctuate in some way.
- Home prices in Hong Kong have fluctuated from month to month in some way.

4 see [witness] a sharp decrease in
- It is expected that we see will a sharp decrease in tax collection due to difficult economic circumstances.
- The increase in the number of lights on the highway will allow us to witness a drastic decrease in traffic accidents.

5 see [witness] a steady increase in
- During the summer season, we saw a steady increase in electricity bills at every branch.
- After the introduction of incentive wages, we witnessed a steady increase in work efficiency.

6 gradual decline
- This green line shows a gradual decline in total revenue over the past ten years.
- The sales figures for men's apparel witnessed a gradual decline while the women's remained the same.

7 decrease drastically
- The number of polar bears decreased drastically in 2017, the hottest year in modern history.
- The voter turnout decreased drastically and, I think, this is because the election was conducted during the peak holiday season.

8 remain steady
- Despite the global recession, South Korea's economic growth is expected to remain steady next year based on the line graph.
- The rate of public transportation usage has remained steady in spite of a significant increase in fares.

03 Presentation (1)

A What's the presentation about?

_____
_____

B Summarize the story and present it to the class.

_____
_____
_____
_____

C Complete the sentences with the phrases in the box.

> · shortfall   · fluctuates   · essence   · balanced

The first graph shows California's state budget in the fiscal year 2016-2017. As you can see, there was a budget (1)_____ of 25 billion dollars. Can you imagine that? 25 billion dollars? How could we have a problem like this? At least on paper, there's this notion that these state budgets are (2)_____. But in reality we haven't had a balanced budget for years. The second graph, which is a line graph, illustrates a troubling trend. The budget shortfall (3)_____ throughout the 1990's, but since 1998, we can see a sharp increase to our current number of 25 billion dollars. As far as we know, the shortfall has increased for various reasons such as pensions and healthcare costs. In (4)_____, there's no real, true balancing going on, and people don't see things that are actually pretty straightforward challenges.

04 Presentation (2)

Give a presentation for five minutes using the slide below.

You are giving a presentation covering statistical analysis of Facebook users in order to figure out a new strategy for marketing. You are comparing users and their ages between two countries. After comparing them, analyze the user trends.

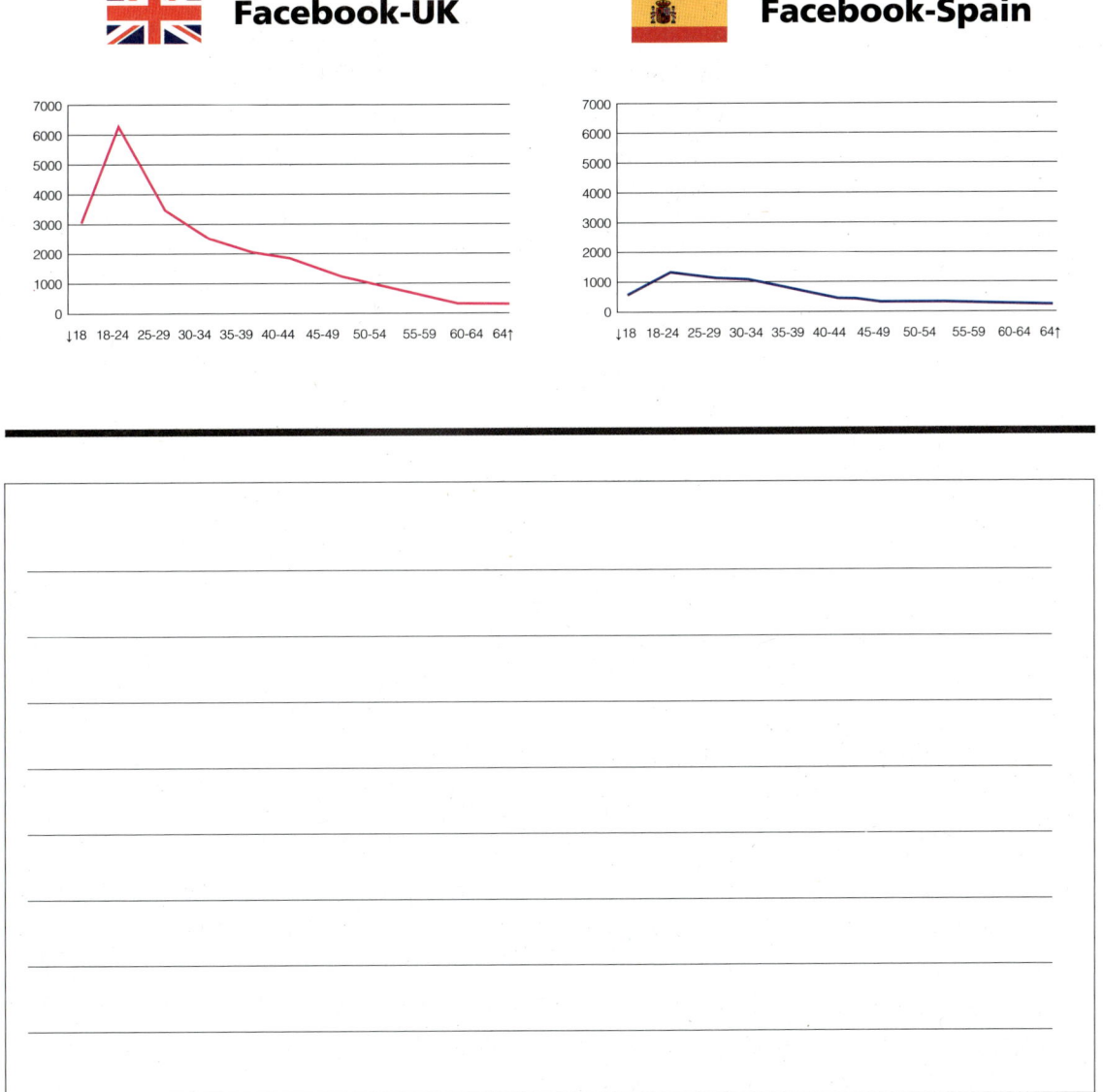

UNIT 13 Describing a Line Graph

05 Sample Presentation

Read the script below aloud with proper rhythm and pronunciation.

Good morning everybody, could I have your attention please. We need to figure out a new marketing strategy for Facebook users. We will look at a statistical analysis based on the following line graphs. According to the information presented in the first graph, it is clear that Facebook is much more popular with the younger generations. The second graph illustrates that the highest number of users are between the ages of 18 and 24. We can also see a sharp decrease in the number of users from ages 25 to 49 and a gradual decline in users from age 50 to 64.

When comparing the two graphs, we can see that the U.K. has a significantly higher number of users than Spain. We have to brainstorm in order to predict future trends so that we may discover a way to increase numbers in Spain within the younger generations and increase the numbers of older users worldwide. The next time we have a look at this analysis, I would like to see a steady increase and a significantly higher number of users, especially from ages 25 to 49.

Presentation Tip

Tell Stories

Human beings are programmed to respond to stories. Stories help us to pay attention, and also to remember things. If you can use stories in your presentation, your audience is more likely to engage and to remember your points afterwards. It is a good idea to start with a story. Think about what story you are trying to tell your audience, and create your presentation to tell it.

06 Mr. Q's Presentation

🎧 **Listen to Mr. Q's presentation and answer the questions below.**

1 What is mentioned as the main reason for the company's slump?

    ⓐ Increased competition   ⓑ Growing costs

    ⓒ Unsatisfied customers   ⓓ Closing stores

2 What do the graphs show about the company?

    ⓐ Its location   ⓑ Its weak points

    ⓒ Its vision   ⓓ Its annual events

3 What are the participants most likely to do next?

_____

_____

_____

BUSINESS JOKES

I met a good friend while taking my morning walk. "Hey Paul, why do you look so dejected today?" "Oh Henry, I'm in trouble. I need cash for the business and have no idea where to get it from!" "Oh I'm sure glad to hear that" I replied. "I was afraid you might think you could borrow it from me!"

07 Exercise

A Underline the best word to complete each sentence.

1 After the replacement of old air purifiers, we (witnessed / withdrew) an increase in air quality.

2 This chart describes several important political trends that (laid / led) to the Great War.

B Fill in the blanks with the given words.

| • obscure | • gradual | • turnover |
| • steady | • disconcerting | • depiction |

1 This line graph uses such _____ data that this is likely the first time this problem has been visualized.

2 This year's budget has been significantly reduced, which is completely _____ to all in the department.

3 These two graphs will provide a _____ of environmental hazards and several potential risks they pose.

4 The annual _____ seems to have fallen short of our expectation.

C Fill in the blanks with the given words.

- declined drastically after
- the first graph illustrates
- is likely to fluctuate in some way
- to be one of the contributing factors

1 _____ the trend of tablet PC sales worldwide.

2 The number of customer complaints _____ we began to implement a new quality control policy last June.

3 Apple's own design appears _____ to its global popularity.

4 The New York stock market _____ at the news that Saudi Arabia may cut its oil production.

Unit 14

Describing a Pie Chart

 **Warm-up**

1. When have you used pie charts? For what kind of data did you use them? Was it successful in getting your message across?

2. What kinds of data lend themselves to being reprsented as parts of a hole?

01 Vocabulary

A Word Definition
Underline the word with the given definition.

1 an amount of money that a business has lost in a particular period of time

   The trade **deficit** is widening due to increasing raw material costs.

2 a period of time when an economy or industry is doing badly

   The government proposed aggressive economic stimulus packages to pull the country out of the prolonged **recession**.

3 not yet used, dealt with, or resolved

   Data from our central servers were analyzed by our security experts and all **remaining** data were done by subcontractors.

4 to take action or make changes that have been officially decided

   Some businesses could suffer from the latest deregulatory policy to be **implemented**.

B Word Use
Write your own sentence using the underlined word in the sentence.

1 Russians **account for** about 5.5 percent of the population.

   _____

2 This acquisition is predicted to **bring in** at least $5 billion in revenue.

   _____

3 Based on the figures in those charts, we can see the company is financially **sound**.

   _____

4 Taking the initiative on this project will strengthen our department's **standing**.

   _____

02 Expression

A Key Expressions

1 <u>These pie charts compare</u>
- These pie charts compare water consumption in Seattle and Los Angeles last year.
- These pie charts compare the use of electricity in the business districts and in the residential areas.

2 <u>account for one third of the total</u>
- Economics books account for one third of the total released by ETA Publishers last month.
- Laptops accounted for one third of the total sales in our electronics store in February.

3 <u>is two times higher [lower] than</u>
- Consumption of beer was two times higher than that of water in the U.K. last quarter.
- Bus fares are two times lower than those of cabs in many cities.

4 <u>make up</u>
- Our guest houses are generally made up of two bedrooms.
- Revenue from tourism makes up 60% of the gross domestic income in Bali.

5 <u>have [account for] the highest percentage of</u>
- Internet use accounts for the highest percentage of what people do in their free time.
- Medical expenses account for the highest percentage of family expenditures for couples over 80.

6 <u>come in at second place</u>
- Food expenses come in at second place in university students' expenditures.
- Russia comes in at second place after Saudi Arabia in oil exports.

7 <u>show a large chunk of</u>
- This pie chart shows a large chunk of camera market share belongs to Canon.
- The pie chart on the top shows engineering to be the most popular major among university students.

8 <u>be rounded off to the nearest 10</u>
- The output of tested engines is rounded off to the nearest 10.
- Regional plastic recycling rates indicated on the pie chart are rounded off to the nearest 10.

03 Presentation (1)

A What's the presentation about?

_____

_____

B Summarize the story and present it to the class.

_____

_____

_____

_____

C Complete the sentences with the phrases in the box.

- revenue   · compare   · recession   · accounts

Let's get this straight. The U.S. economy is big. It boasted a GDP of $14.7 trillion in 2010. Now, out of that pie, the government spends 36%. It can easily be seen from the second pie chart that this (1)_____ for more than one third of the total GDP. This amount is being spent on healthcare, pensions, and other forms of social security. These pie charts (2)_____ three different types of spending: federal, state, and local.

As you can see, we're spending 36 percent. This raises an important question: how much are we bringing in through taxes? The tax (3)_____ accounts for just 26 percent. Now this leaves a 10 percent deficit, which is a mind-blowing number. The third pie chart clearly shows a large chunk of deficit. The biggest reason for the significant deficit is the (4)_____, and it has been growing for quite a while now.

04 Presentation (2)

Give a presentation for five minutes using the slide below.

This is a part of the strategic analysis for a new marketing campaign. Through analysis of the following pie charts, you are going to explain the current state of the market between search engines and stress the importance of a new marketing strategy to gain control of the search engine market.

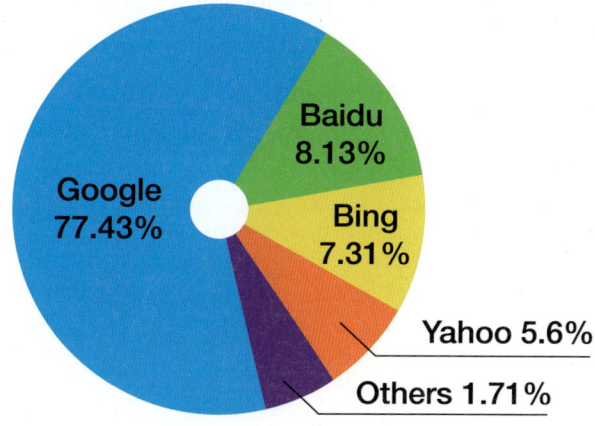

05 Sample Presentation

Read the script below aloud with proper rhythm and pronunciation.

Good morning everyone. Today we are going to discuss the importance of gaining control of the search engine market through analysis of the following pie chart. This chart compares different search engines represented by color and percentage. From the figures, you can see that Google has the highest percentage of market share with 49% while the remaining 51% is shared between other search engines. The data obtained for this analysis is the result of the accumulated time and effort made by our marketing team.

They have suggested the need for a new marketing strategy in order for us to gain an upper hand. The data is accurate, so we know exactly where we stand compared to individual companies. The chart shows that Yahoo comes in at second place, but they only maintain 50% of what Google is holding, which shows that Google's market share is two times higher than their nearest competitor.

Presentation Tip

Use Your Voice Effectively

The spoken word is actually a pretty inefficient means of communication, because it uses only one of your audience's five senses. That's why presenters tend to use visual aids, too. But you can help to make the spoken word better by using your voice effectively. Varying the speed at which you talk, and emphasizing changes in pitch and tone all help to make your voice more interesting and hold your audience's attention.

06 Mr. Q's Presentation

🎧 **Listen to Mr. Q's presentation and answer the questions below.**

1 What are being compared in the presentation?

   ⓐ Search engines ⓑ Web developers

   ⓒ Advertising agencies ⓓ Supermarkets

2 According to the graph and table, what can be inferred about Google?

   ⓐ It is the second largest search engine.

   ⓑ Its share in the market is more than 50%.

   ⓒ Its market share is almost twice that of Yahoo.

   ⓓ It lost 20% of its market to its biggest competitor.

3 What is indicated about the next meeting?

   _____

   _____

   _____

BUSINESS JOKES

This is the story of four people named Everybody, Somebody, Anybody, and Nobody. There was an important job to be done and Everybody was asked to do it. Anybody could have done it, but Nobody did it. Somebody got angry about that, because it was Everybody's job. Everybody thought Anybody could do it, but Nobody realized that Everybody wouldn't do it.

07 Exercise

A Underline the best word to complete each sentence.

1 It looks like our charity drive will (break / bring) in more than two million dollars.
2 Only 45% of those surveyed responded positively to the design, while the (remaining / reminding) 55% gave harsh comments about it.

B Fill in the blanks with the given words.

- implement
- pitfall
- standing
- deficit
- expenditure
- sound

1 We will need more funding to properly _____ a much more aggressive marketing campaign.
2 Most of the budget _____ comes from social security costs.
3 This new technology will enhance our _____ in the mobile communication industry.
4 We should obtain data from _____ resources for accuracy's sake.

C Fill in the blanks with the given words.

- accounted for two-thirds of
- are about three times higher
- comes in at second place
- were rounded off to

1 Texas _____ for most populous U.S. state.
2 This item _____ the total sales last month.
3 Coffee prices in a cafe _____ than those of canned products.
4 All data presented on the pie chart _____ the nearest 10 for figures over 1,000.

114 BUSINESS INTERACTION *Presentation*

Actual Case 3

Art of the Interface

Krystal Lauk

Krystal Lauk debunks the myth that illustrators all work on children's books and gives a 5-minute glimpse into the world of art and technology.

Unit 15

01 Vocabulary

A Word Definition
Underline the word with the given definition.

1 having an extremely strong desire to do or have a lot of something

   She had a **voracious** appetite for knowledge.

2 an idea which is wrong or untrue, but which people believe because they do not understand the subject properly

   Believing that the world under the sea is silent is a common **misconception**.

3 unusual or strange and often amusing

   The actress was funny and **whimsical** in her first comedy role.

4 work or repairs that make a building or place look newer or better

   They said the building, which was completed in 1923, needed a **facelift**.

B Word Use
Write your own sentence using the underlined word in the sentence.

1 I feel quite **nostalgic** for the place where I grew up.

   _____

2 His mind was like a sponge, ready to **absorb** anything.

   _____

3 Our modern society is full of cultural **diversity**.

   _____

4 Debbie hopes that her movie will **inspire** others to travel.

   _____

02 Presentation

Watch the presentation and answer the questions below.

 Krystal Lauk is an illustrator working for Google play. She talks about how illustrators are perceived as and explains what illustrators do. She concludes the talk by how illustrations fit in modern society in conjunction to technology.

* Video may not be available depending on the connection to Youtube

A What's the presentation about?

_____
_____

B What's the purpose of this presentation?

_____
_____

C Summarize the story and present it to the class.

_____
_____
_____
_____
_____
_____

03 Transcript

Watch the presentation again and fill in the blanks with the words in the box.

Well, hi there. I'm Krystal. I'm an illustrator on Google Play and have also worked with clients such as Facebook, Uber, UC Berkeley, and Fast Company. So, from an early age I had such a voracious (1)_____ for art and drawing. And my parents definitely feared that they had a starving artist on their hands. But what they didn't realize was that there's actually more opportunity than ever for artists. Especially, namely illustration. Illustration is basically the bridge between (2)_____ communication and art, and it has a lot of value especially in today's tech-driven world.

But being said that, there's still a lot of misconceptions around where illustration actually belongs in the world. When I tell people I'm an illustrator, for example, a lot of times I'll get the response, "oh, like children's books?" And there's a reason why that's such a common response. Illustration has such a nostalgic value. Likely the first content that you ever picked up was a picture book. And thinking about today and the Internet, so much of our communication and the way we (3)_____ information and buy products all happens digitally. And so our digital lives have truly become an extension of ourselves.

And while all the technical kinks have been worked out, where's the emotive value, you know, where's the humanity in all of it? Illustration has always been a tool for storytelling. And storytelling has remained one of the most powerful tools for human communication since basically the dawn of time. But what I love so much about today's world is that we are so hyper-connected, we're on a global scale. And, you know, everybody is in the story. Everyone is included in this story. And illustration can really serve to celebrate diversity in cultures in a very (4)_____, sincere way.

But illustration doesn't just have to be consumer-facing. For Uber, for example, I actually did storyboarding that inspires product design. So kind of using these new ways. So illustration is great for storytelling but it can actually serve as the (5)_____ of your brand. At

BUSINESS INTERACTION *Presentation*

Google for example, delight is a huge word and it's such a big part of their brand values. And you know with delight it elevates your wellbeing and, you know, creates a positive perception of the world, and illustration is at the heart of that.

Casper is a great example, breaking out of commoditization and using illustration to (6)_____ that in a really whimsical way. Uber recently just had a facelift where they use illustration to really create a richness that carries across, you know, different cultures all around the world. And companies are even inviting users to express themselves through illustration or even create it themselves. Like Airbnb Create or the new Google Allo or Facebook Messenger.

And as our products become more and more complex, illustration can actually serve as a way to create a simple more (7)_____ experience, a way of understanding. And so that's an example from Google G Suite. And you know we're always absorbing information and sharing it with our friends and of course illustrated infographics are the perfect way to do that. Easy to absorb and share with our friends.

So as you can see, there's actually a lot of opportunity for creatives in illustration. You know we're not only in this age of technology but we're in an age of creativity as well. And when you know something like illustration and technology play together amazing things happen. Great human, genuine experiences.

So next time you're drumming up that next marketing (8)_____ or brand refresh, go hire an illustrator. You'll be glad you did.
Thank you.

07 Exercise

A Underline the best word to complete each sentence.

1 Our digital lives have become an (explosion / extension) of ourselves.

2 It is a (misconception / misconduct) that Heather was fabulously wealthy.

B Fill in the blanks with the given words.

| • serve | • absorb | • inspired |
| • diversity | • approachable | • nostalgic |

1 Many people are _____ for the good old days.

2 Black walls _____ a lot of heat during the day.

3 After all, _____ is what helps us to grow and change.

4 It was her work that _____ my research in the first place.

C Fill in the blanks with the given words.

- to drum up our business
- on our hands
- was the perfect way to
- is such a big part of

1 We may have a bit of a problem _____.

2 Training _____ my life, I can't imagine life without it.

3 It _____ celebrate Independence Day.

4 Could you find another way _____?

Unit 16

Highlighting Information

 **Warm-up**

1. There are a variety of ways to highlight information in a presentation. What purposes do you need to highlight information for?

2. How do you prefer to highlight information in your presentation? In what way do you think it is effective and useful? Share your experience with the class.

01 Vocabulary

A Word Definition
Underline the word with the given definition.

1 the quality of being suited to serve a purpose well; practicality

   We guarantee that customers will be satisfied with the easy installation and high functionality of this software.

2 a part of an area of activity, especially of business, trade etc.

   Three of seven sectors have shown negative growth in the last two years.

3 having official approval to do something, especially because of having reached an acceptable standard

   The auditing process is how all state universities are accredited to confer degrees.

4 to talk too proudly about your abilities, achievements, or possessions

   The buffet boasts a broad range of cuisines from France, Italy, and Japan.

B Word Use
Write your own sentence using the underlined word in the sentence.

1 Some faulty reports about our next model are **floating** around on the Internet.

   _____

2 Customers will soon **get a feel for** how useful this application is for increasing their daily productivity.

   _____

3 The company is **partnering with** businesses from China, India, and Turkey.

   _____

4 We may **source** this material by tracking its manufacturer's number.

   _____

02 Expression

A Key Expressions

1 it is a known fact that
- It is a known fact that I am an extremely experienced developer who can build a whole website independently.
- It is a known fact that the government's economic policies have changed pretty frequently.

2 a point often overlooked
- A key point often overlooked in communication is listening carefully to the other party.
- Another point often overlooked by start-up business owners is the importance of benchmarking.

3 without a doubt
- After reviewing their earnings reports from the past few years, we have found that the company is, without a doubt, financially stable.
- The accident was, without a doubt, caused by the loose security policy.

4 I must say (that)
- I must say there are no security problems with this software.
- I must say that the board already passed this investment proposal in early June.

5 with this in mind
- The bank typically accepts loan applications from small businesses. With this in mind, we are likely to secure urgent funding this time.
- With the normal summer requests in mind, we should prepare at least 100 units per day.

6 the first thing to remember
- The first thing to remember when you meet investors is to show your understanding of their particular business interest.
- The first thing to remember for your job interview is to stay confident.

7 we have to ask ourselves
- We have to ask ourselves what the reason is for a recent decrease in customer visits.
- It is time we have to ask ourselves how we can overcome such a prolonged, sluggish business environment.

8 point out
- I would like to point out that there was a significant loss in every service division in August.
- The manager pointed out that most technical problems reported in the early stages were resolved.

03 Presentation (1)

A What's the presentation about?

_____

_____

B Summarize the story and present it to the class.

_____

_____

_____

_____

C Complete the sentences with the phrases in the box.

> · functionality   · point   · expected   · bet

Now, I want to (1)_____ something out here. It is a known fact that the thickest part of the MaxioFeather is still thinner than the thinnest part of the Webzin series. How did we make it thinner than the Webzin? Wasn't it enough to make the product look better? See how it can fit inside one of these envelopes that are always floating around the office? In fact, there's one in this envelope here...

This is it. This is what it looks like. This is the new MaxioFeather. You can get a feel for how thin it is. I (2)_____ that it is as thin as the mobile phone you have in your pocket. I must say there is no loss of (3)_____ with its smaller size. All the software systems have even been upgraded. Is it better than what you (4)_____? It has a full-size keyboard and a full HD OLED display. Isn't it amazing?

04 Presentation (2)

Give a presentation for five minutes using the slide below.

You are giving a presentation about a new notebook from your company. It is so thin and small that people can carry it with them, even in the envelope pictured below.
Emphasize the thinness as its defining feature and give some additional information about the new notebook: Be sure to mention the full-size keyboard and display.

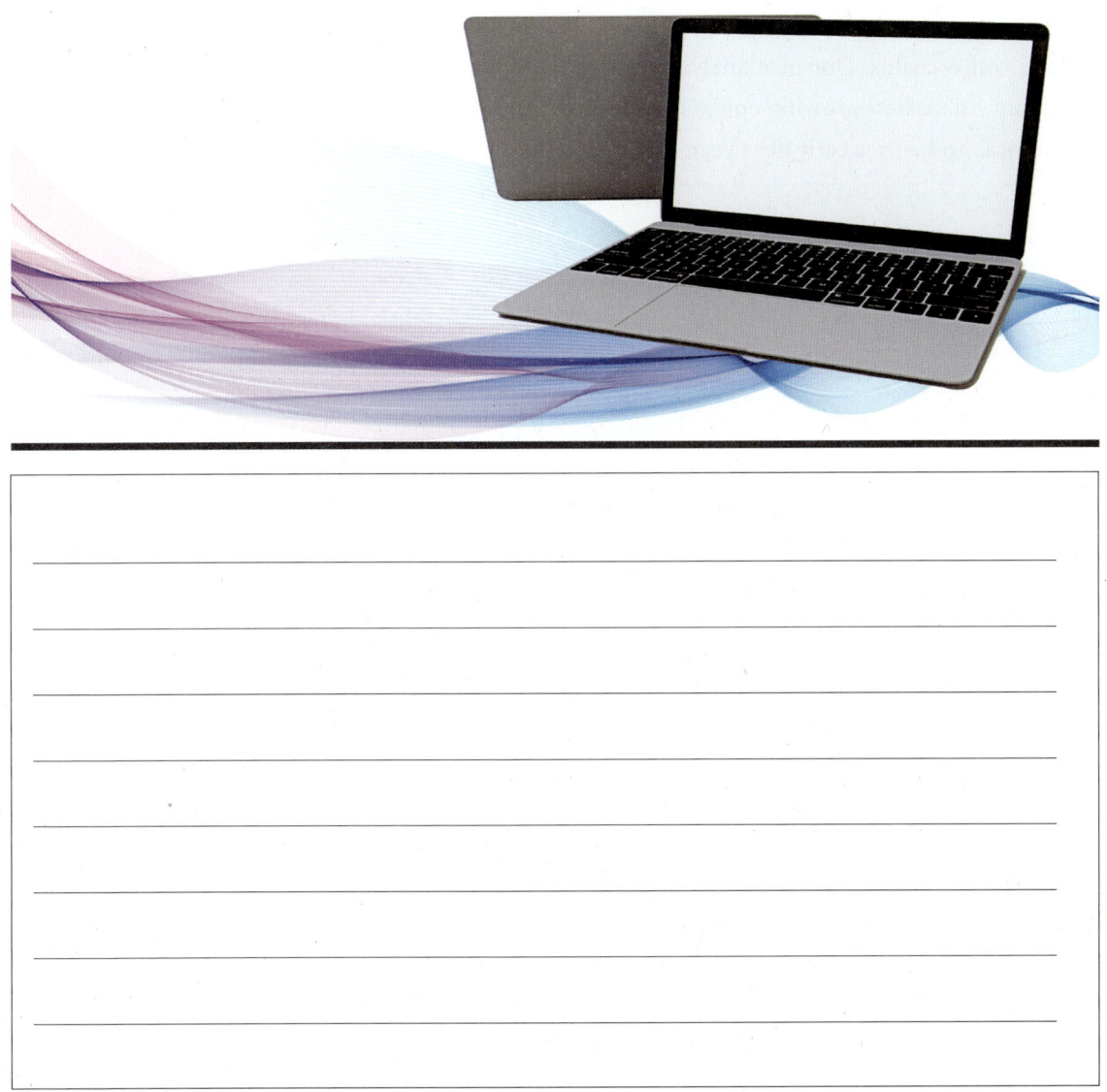

05 Sample Presentation

Read the script below aloud with proper rhythm and pronunciation.

> Our presentation today will cover the various international operations and partnerships of Star Coffee. I would like to start by drawing your attention to the table on page number two. I must say you will be surprised to see that coffee stores in Australia, Thailand and the U.K. have not partnered with any big franchises and they are mostly owned by individuals. I would also like to point out that there has been considerable growth in all sectors from 2017 to 2018. We have to ask ourselves what the reason is for this worldwide growth.
>
> The rapid growth was unexpected and this can be credited to Star Coffee sourcing their beans from Kenya, which allowed them to import their beans at a much lower cost than some of the other coffee chains. Our new analysis has led us to the conclusion that Star Coffee is, without a doubt, the fastest growing coffee franchise in the world with new openings planned for the Americas and Africa early next year.

Presentation Tip

Use Your Body

It has been estimated that more than three quarters of communication is non-verbal. That means that as well as your tone of voice, your body language is crucial to getting your message across. Make your gestures open and confident, and move naturally around the stage.

06 Mr. Q's Presentation

🎧 **Listen to Mr. Q's presentation and answer the questions below.**

1 What country boasts the most coffee shops on average?

ⓐ U.K.   ⓑ U.S.

ⓒ Japan   ⓓ Korea

2 What franchise has over 600 locations in Korea?

ⓐ Star Coffee   ⓑ Starbucks

ⓒ Tom's Coffee   ⓓ Dunkin' Donuts

3 According to the speaker, what is the reason for the boom of coffee shops?

_____

_____

_____

BUSINESS JOKES

The banker fell overboard from a friend's sailboat. The friend grabbed a life preserver, held it up, not knowing if the banker could swim, and shouted, "Can you float alone?" "Obviously," the banker replied, "but this is a heck of a time to talk business."

07 Exercise

A Underline the best word to complete each sentence.

1 This car accident was, without a (doubt / duty), caused by recklessness.
2 With rising oil prices (involve / in mind), we'd better limit our production to 100 tons per month.

B Fill in the blanks with the given words.

- guarantee
- credited
- sources
- division
- functionality
- boasts

1 We will be focusing on both prices and technical _____.
2 The hotel chain _____ superb food exclusively supplied by local restaurants.
3 The grocery chain _____ their products directly from local organic farms.
4 The success of our new product is _____ to its innovative design by Jonna Wesley.

C Fill in the blanks with the given words.

- often overlooked in a debate
- the first thing to remember when
- we have to ask ourselves
- can get a feel for

1 A fact _____ is that you are there to sell your point.
2 You now probably _____ what most start-up businesses experience in the very early stages.
3 _____ writing a résumé is to keep it organized.
4 _____ what the reason is for the constant decreases in our sales.

Unit 17

Summarizing the Main Points

 **Warm-up**

1. Have you ever been in a hurry to finish a presentation in time? How did it happen? What do you think is the purpose of summarizing the points?

2. Do you think it would be OK to finish the presentation without summarizing the main points? How would you allocate time between the summarization and the rest of the population.

01 Vocabulary

A Word Definition
Underline the word with the given definition.

1 happening or developing gradually over a period of time

The apparel company announced that there has been progressive growth in their international transactions.

2 just; only

Merely advertising products on SNS is not likely to guarantee commercial success.

3 to make a formal, usually public, promise that you will do something

The new CEO has pledged to reform the organization without compromising employee morale.

4 to prefer someone or something to other things or people

Becker's design, favored by the majority, was finally selected as the new company logo.

B Word Use
Write your own sentence using the underlined word in the sentence.

1 In order to achieve our primary objective, the marketing and engineering departments should work **hand in hand**.

_____

2 Sigma Electronics is conducting a campaign to encourage people to **trade in** their old computer for a new one.

_____

3 Many automobile manufacturers started to launch **fuel-efficient**, low-emission cars.

_____

4 We need a new strategy which can help us stay ahead of the **market forces** in this field.

_____

02 Expression

A Key Expressions

1 near the end of my presentation
- Now we are nearing the end of my presentation.
- Please think about what you want to ask me in the Q&A session as I'm nearing the end of my presentation.

2 conclude by summarizing
- The presenter concluded by summarizing what we need to further in order to solve the current issue.
- The article concluded by summarizing famous advertising strategies the company used in the past.

3 run through
- Let me quickly run through the first process again before entering into the second.
- Current savings procedures are not effective, as we are running through raw materials at a greater rate than expected.

4 you have just learned
- You have just learned how the rainforests were formed.
- Use the information you have just learned to solve the following problem.

5 In conclusion
- In conclusion, there is an immediate need for emergency shelters in the affected area.
- In conclusion, our endeavor to develop this product was financially reasonable and a valuable experience.

6 on the whole
- On the whole, Blue Dog Beverage saw a decline in sales last year.
- On the whole, this magazine contributes to raising public awareness for cancer prevention.

7 All things considered
- All things considered, more promising projects will receive more funding.
- All things considered, properties on a two-year lease in the area will not stay on the market for more than two weeks on average.

8 leave you with one thought
- In closing, I would like to leave you with one thought: the harder you work, the better the results.
- If I can leave you with one thought, it is that you should not rely solely on the Internet as a resource.

UNIT 17 Summarizing the Main Points

03 Presentation (1)

A What's the presentation about?

_____

_____

B Summarize the story and present it to the class.

_____

_____

_____

_____

C Complete the sentences with the phrases in the box.

> · diversity   · progressive   · considered   · summarizing

Let me conclude by (1)_____ what we introduced today. We've proudly disclosed the MaxFeather and added the Maxreen to our already strong lineup of MaxTech TV and Maxio products. Some people might think that Maxreen is the only computer of the line, right? The other products are an MP3 player, a TV, and a smartphone. We realized this as well and decided that our company's name should reflect this (2)_____ a little bit more.

So we're announcing today that we're dropping the word "Computer" from our name. From now on, we'll be known as simply MaxTech Inc. You know, I was so excited about this announcement because this change of name represents our (3)_____ growth as a global company. All things (4)_____, we are an integrated corporation and not merely a computer company. I really believe the two products we unveiled today will be significant in continuing that growth.

04 Presentation (2)

Give a presentation for five minutes using the slide below.

You just finished a presentation about the statistical analysis of trends in the mobile market in order to suggest a new marketing strategy. You will summarize your presentation with the three main points in the slide. Using supportive statements, give a clear and short summarization.

Takeaways

The mobile media market in Europe is growing rapidly
- App and browsing usage is creating ever more opportunities for consumer engagement
- Don't assume it is all about apps on only the iPhone!

Consider carefully the mobile audience you wish to reach
- Identity which media they engage with, how, and through which devices
- Robust market intelligence data adds value to product and campain planning & targeting
- The reality, as revealed by measurement, is often different from intuition

Don't get left behind on mobile
- A complate picture of the mobile media market means no chance of being blindsided

---

UNIT 17 Summarizing the Main Points

05 Sample Presentation

Read the script below aloud with proper rhythm and pronunciation.

Now that I am nearing the end of my presentation, I would like to conclude by summarizing the takeaways from today's presentation. For one, mobile media in Europe is growing rapidly. We need to take advantage of this as it's a potentially huge market. The second is that you need to consider the mobile audience you wish to reach. Identify what media they engage with and what types of devices they use.

On the whole, you need to come up with an effective marketing strategy so that you don't get left behind in the rapidly changing smartphone market. I can't stress this enough but it is absolutely essential that you have a sound marketing strategy to succeed in this industry.

Presentation Tip

Courteous, Gracious, Professional

When audience members ask questions or give comments, you should be gracious and thank them for their input. Even if someone is being difficult, you must keep to the high ground and at all times be a gentleman or lady and courteously deal with such individuals. The true professional can always remain cool and in control. Remember, it is your reputation, so always remain gracious even with the most challenging of audiences.

06　Mr. Q's Presentation

🎧 **Listen to Mr. Q's presentation and answer the questions below.**

1 What is the speaker summarizing?

    ⓐ Long-term goals   ⓑ Key issues

    ⓒ Company rules   ⓓ Election results

2 According to the speaker, what two areas are closely related?

    ⓐ Marketing and sales   ⓑ Marketing and research

    ⓒ Sales and public relations   ⓓ Research and purchasing

3 According to the speaker, what is needed to achieve their goals?

_____

_____

_____

BUSINESS JOKES

The boss called one of his employees into the office.
"Rob," he said, "you've been with the company for a year. You started off in the post room, and one month after that you were promoted to vice-chairman."
"Now I want you to take over the company. What do you say to that?" The employee said, "Thanks, Dad."

UNIT 17　Summarizing the Main Points

07 Exercise

A Underline the best word to complete each sentence.

1 (Surely / Merely) advertising on TV is not a good way to ensure a successful publicity campaign.

2 The Apple founder created the market (force / form) necessary to influence the music industry with the iPod.

B Fill in the blanks with the given words.

| • progressive | • dominant | • concluded |
| • pledged | • favored | • investigate |

1 All board members _____ to begin a reform effort without further delay.

2 The foundation has been making a _____ effort to achieve economic independence in the region.

3 The writer's latest novel was not _____ by critics mostly because of the poor plot.

4 The speaker _____ by summarizing what else we need to think about to protect the environment.

C Fill in the blanks with the given words.

- on the whole
- you have just learned
- in order to achieve our goals
- let me quickly run through

1 _____, the board and the accounting department should work hand in hand.

2 _____ how our ecosystem and economy can both flourish.

3 _____, this magazine deals with the rising public awareness of forest conservation.

4 _____ all the ideas we have discussed before proceeding to a final decision.

Unit 18

Closing a Presentation

 Warm-up

1 It is important to give a memorable final impression in order to highlight and characterize your main points. What do you think is the most impressive closing for a presentation?

2 Recommend an unforgettable closing based on your experience and share it with the class.

01 Vocabulary

A Word Definition
Underline the word with the given definition.

1 hard work or effort that someone puts into a particular activity because they care about it a lot

   Please accept this as a way of thanking you for your hard work and dedication over the last two years.

2 to succeed in achieving something after trying for a long time

   The mobile division has attained the highest rank in customer satisfaction.

3 an attempt to do something new or difficult

   I hope your endeavors in building sound partnerships with larger companies throughout Europe are successful.

4 the control of a group of people or a situation

   Mr. Park took command as construction manager, asking everyone to leave the demolition site.

B Word Use
Write your own sentence using the underlined word in the sentence.

1 The new manager, Stephen Harris, said scheduling work shifts in both a productive and fair way is pretty **tough** on him.

   _____

2 The consultant recommended we implement a **restructuring** of the company, at least at the management level.

   _____

3 The company's sales target received a **downward** revision from Jefferies' analyst Howard Ruben after the severe financial crisis.

   _____

4 It is expected that this upward **spiral** of growth will continue thanks to their flexible financial policy.

   _____

02 Expression

A Key Expressions

1 I hope I have convinced you that
- I hope I have convinced you that the MADE program is worth a try at your young age.
- I hope I have convinced you that this investment is a great opportunity to expand your business territory.

2 overrun my allotted time
- I'm afraid I'm about to overrun my allotted time, so I will only remind you of the key points.
- Let me conclude my presentation at this point since I've overrun my allotted time already.

3 bring my presentation to a close
- Let me explain only one more thing before I bring my presentation to a close.
- I was going to bring my presentation to a close when the CEO showed up in the meeting room.

4 strongly recommend that
- I strongly recommend that you make some time your self and don't solely devote your time to work.
- I strongly recommend that you register for this year's Design Conference as soon as possible since there is limited seating.

5 I'd like to leave you with the words
- Last, I'd like to leave you with the words "Will is power."
- I'd like to leave you with the words "Accept responsibility for your life. Know that it is you who will get you where you want to go, no one else." Thank you.

6 remember what I said
- Please remember what I said about the key points for online marketing.
- Try to remember what I said today when you start planning your business.

7 Mark my words
- Mark my words, appropriate behavior is essential at all times.
- Mark my words and make use of it for your project.

8 To put it into the words of
- To put it into the words of Albert Einstein, "I am thankful for all of those who said no to me. It's because of them I'm doing it myself."
- To put it into the words of Frank Sinatra, "The best revenge is massive success."

03 Presentation (1)

A What's the presentation about?

_____
_____

B Summarize the story and present it to the class.

_____
_____
_____
_____

C Complete the sentences with the phrases in the box.

- simpler   · close   · recommend   · affected

Now before I bring my presentation to a (1)_____ I would like to talk about something that I saw when I was young which (2)_____ me profoundly. It was the mid-1980's, computers were just starting to get stylish, and I was just starting out in the world. It was much (3)_____ back in those days as there were no cell phones, tablets or any of that stuff.

I was once reading a news magazine that I liked. In the middle of it was an ad with a man saying goodbye to his college-age son. It was very touching, to say the least. Below was the man's final message to his son, "Stay hungry, stay foolish." It got me thinking because I wasn't aware what the words hungry and foolish really meant there. I strongly (4)_____ that you think about it because it can change your life forever. So I' like to leave you with the words "Stay hungry, stay foolish." Thank you.

04 Presentation (2)

Give a presentation for five minutes using the slide below.

You gave a presentation about the importance of social media in order convince people associated with the hotel industry of the necessity of an online presence. It is time to close your presentation now. Using the following slide, give a memorable statement about your company as you close your presentation.

Thank You

Please feel free to contact us to inquire about our services, including speaking engagements.

05 Sample Presentation

Read the script below aloud with proper rhythm and pronunciation.

So I strongly recommend that you remember your time spent here at this university, for now life truly begins. If you think your professors were tough on you, just wait until you have a boss. Mark my words, ladies and gentlemen. It doesn't get easier, but with the hard work and dedication you have put in over the past years and the degrees you have attained, it will certainly be less painful. I would like to leave you with the words of Dhirubhai Ambani who said "If you don't build your dream, someone else will hire you to help them build theirs." Remember what I said in the beginning of my talk today, "No pain, no gain." Thank you all and good luck with your future endeavors.

Presentation Tip

Finish Strong

Think of yourself as an attorney arguing a case in front of the jury. Structure your closing statements the way a lawyer would—with flair and gravity. Once you've delivered your final, impactful line, don't say "thank you" right away. Instead, wait six or seven seconds and then say, "I'm happy to take questions."

06 Mr. Q's Presentation

🎧 **Listen to Mr. Q's presentation and answer the questions below.**

1 According to the speaker what needs to be done?

ⓐ Expanding   ⓑ Advertising

ⓒ Restructuring   ⓓ Recruiting

2 What does the speaker predict will happen if nothing is done?

ⓐ The company will prosper.   ⓑ The company will close.

ⓒ The company will be renovated.   ⓓ The company will stagnate.

3 What do you think the speaker means by the word "the time is now"?

_____

_____

_____

BUSINESS JOKES

I work in a busy office, so when a computer goes down it causes quite an inconvenience. Recently one of our computers not only crashed, it made a noise that sounded like a heart monitor. "This computer has flat-lined," a co-worker called out with mock horror. "Does anyone here know how to do mouse-to-mouse?"

 **Exercise**

A Underline the best word to complete each sentence.

1. Mostly because of the bribery case surrounding the CEO, the stock price of Blue Ridge Railway is in a (forward / downward) spiral.
2. The revised traffic law is very (naive / tough) on drunk drivers, imposing heavier fines, for instance.

B Fill in the blanks with the given words.

- endeavors
- command
- allotted
- recommend
- attained
- convinced

1. I am looking forward to meeting you to discuss cooperative _____ between the two companies.
2. I don't think our yearly sales target can be _____ easily with the current market situation.
3. I hope I have _____ you that this internship program is beneficial to both the company and the participants.
4. Mr. Norman took _____ as site manager, replacing Mr. Johnson who retired last week.

C Fill in the blanks with the given words.

- mark my words, please
- thank you for the hard work and dedication
- I strongly recommend
- let me bring my presentation to a close

1. _____ you make spare time for your family and friends.
2. _____ you have put into the completion of this project.
3. _____ at this point since I'm about to overrun my allotted time.
4. _____. When it comes to doing business, honesty is vital at all times.

Unit 19

Handling the Q&A Session

 **Warm-up**

1. Have you ever gotten unexpected questions from the audience after your presentation? How did you handle them? Share your experience in detail with the class.

2. Suppose that you have a presentation related to your work. What kind of questions do you think will be dealt with during the Q&A session after your presentation? Why are you expecting those questions?

01 Vocabulary

A Word Definition
Underline the word with the given definition.

1 to say or write something again using different words to express what you mean in a way that is clearer or more acceptable

   Sara McKay always rephrases and double-checks a question before answering it.

2 a feeling of anger because something has happened that you think is unfair

   Unilateral decisions by the boss are likely to arouse resentment among the staff.

3 a lucky or successful situation where people can make a lot of money

   Hotels are expecting a bonanza during the two-week International Electronics Expo in Busan.

4 a task that is taken on

   The construction company was chosen for a huge undertaking: building a canal through the city.

B Word Use
Write your own sentence using the underlined word in the sentence.

1 The reviewer **broke down** people's reactions to the new movie into positive and negative.

   _____

2 Speculations about her incompetence at work were **put to rest** after she closed a successful deal.

   _____

3 You have to include any possible **hidden costs** in the budget plan.

   _____

4 The new director has been given **carte blanche** to manage every financial transaction in the corporation.

   _____

02 Expression

A Key Expressions

1 move on to the Q&A session
- Now let me move on to the Q&A session.
- In this presentation, we will first review a financial report and discuss new business strategies, and then we will move on to the Q&A session.

2 keep one's questions till
- Please keep your questions till the Q&A session.
- Keep your questions till I ask for them at the end of this presentation, please.

3 any questions concerning
- If you have any questions concerning today's topic, ask me without hesitation.
- Do you have any questions concerning the three popular marketing strategies we discussed today?

4 if any of you have further questions
- If any of you have further questions, you may refer to the handouts on the desk.
- Ask my assistant later if any of you have further questions.

5 did I address your concerns
- Through this presentation, did I address your concerns over food safety?
- Did I address your growing concerns about the budget deficit?

6 please fire away
- If you have any questions about the performance of this new machine, please fire away.
- Please fire away about our vacation policy, or anything else you need to know.

7 rephrase one's question
- If I could just rephrase your question, you would like to know if there are any limitations to using the office building's parking lot.
- Let me rephrase your question. You asked me how to apply for a mortgage, didn't you?

8 not in a position to answer
- I am afraid I am not in a position to answer that question.
- Honestly, we are not in a position to answer those kinds of questions.

03 Presentation (1)

A What's the presentation about?

_____

_____

B Summarize the story and present it to the class.

_____

_____

_____

_____

C Complete the sentences with the phrases in the box.

> • cover   • wrap up   • further   • move on

Unfortunately, it looks like I'm running out of time. I need to (1)_____ my presentation. There were a few more slides I wasn't able to (2)_____, but if you'd like that information, I will be happy to e-mail them to you. I'd like to thank you all once again for your time, and now let's (3)_____ to the Q&A session. If you have any questions or comments, please raise your hand. We have a large audience today, and this would be the best way to get to everyone.

All right, ladies and gentlemen, we are out of time, but if any of you have (4)_____ questions, please come and talk to me after the presentation. If you'd like me to e-mail any information, please leave me your business card. Thank you.

04 Presentation (2)

Give a presentation for five minutes using the slide below.

You gave a presentation covering the analysis of Eagle Corp. You have presented all the information you prepared such as products, advertising, market share, business models, competitiveness, and 5-year performance. Now, you will open the floor for questions, if the audience wants to know anything else beyond the information mentioned.

Have we left any questions unanswered?

"The Power of Eagle is Empowerment."

UNIT 19 Handling the Q&A Session

05 Sample Presentation

Read the script below aloud with proper rhythm and pronunciation.

> I thank you all for keeping your questions till the end of this presentation and now I'll be happy to answer any questions you may have. Let's break it down into three categories mentioned in my presentation. Are there any questions concerning market reactions? No? How about surveying techniques for brand recognition? It seems I've managed to put to rest all concerns regarding those two topics.
>
> We have just enough time for a few questions concerning the product itself. Yes? How will the exchange rate affect the pricing? I'm afraid I'm not in a position to answer that question at the moment as we cannot confirm any international orders at this time. Let's discuss that on another occasion, once we have confirmed orders. Does anyone have any final questions? Good, Thank you for your time and let's get back to work.

Presentation Tip

That's a Good Question

You can use statements like, "that's a really good question," or "I'm glad you asked me that," to buy yourself a few moments to organize your response. Will the other people in the audience know you are using these filler sentences to reorder your thoughts? Probably not. And even if they do, it still makes the presentation more smooth than um's and ah's littering your answer.

06 Mr. Q's Presentation

🎧 **Listen to Mr. Q's presentation and answer the questions below.**

1 According to the speaker what doesn't exist?

ⓐ Hidden costs   ⓑ High expenses

ⓒ Deep interest   ⓓ Resentment

2 What was Mr. Waite given for the completion of the project?

ⓐ Sample products   ⓑ Huge funding

ⓒ Enough time   ⓓ Full authority

3 What other questions do you think Mr. Q could get from the audience?

_____

_____

_____

BUSINESS JOKES

A group of colleagues went to a hospital, where one of their team would be having a brain transplant. One of them asked, "What will the cost of a new brain be?" The doctor replied, "A female brain costs $20,000 and a male brain costs $40,000." The men smirked, but one of the females asked, "Why is that, doctor?"
"Well," the doctor replied, "the female brain costs less because it has been used."

07 Exercise

A Underline the best word to complete each sentence.

1 We can put to (least / rest) the concern that we may fail the health inspection.

2 You have to consider all the possible (hidden / hideous) costs when you plan to replace old machinery.

B Fill in the blanks with the given words.

• undertaking	• fire away	• carte blanche
• rephrase	• speculation	• resentment

1 Several contractors are expressing _____ due to the continuously delayed payments.

2 If I could just _____ what you said, you want detailed guidelines for submitting your work to the contest?

3 Please _____ about our company's reward policy.

4 The new CFO has been given _____ to manage the cash flow of the corporation.

C Fill in the blanks with the given words.

- we are going to cover every aspect of
- we are not in a position
- do you have any questions
- broken down into two extreme ends

1 Honestly, _____ to answer your question.

2 During the presentation, _____ the revised health insurance policy, then we will move on to the Q&A session.

3 Since the release of our new SUV model, customer feedback can be _____ _____: excellent and terrible.

4 _____ concerning our plan to expand overseas?

Actual Case 4

Future of Work and Learning

Gary Bolles

Unit 20

Gary Bolles gives us a 5-minute explanation of how rapid technology changes have impacted work and education in our society, and predicts what the future holds.

01 Vocabulary

A Word Definition
Underline the word with the given definition.

1 very great, serious, or important

Seoul requires a **seismic** change in policy if we are to get people out of their cars and on to public transport.

2 to prevent something from continuing in its usual way by causing problems

That might be why he is trying to **disrupt** the amendment procedure.

3 lose or cause to lose moisture or solvent as vapor

Plants keep cool during the summer by **evaporating** water from their leaves.

4 making things happen or change rather than reacting to events

There needs to be positive action and **proactive** measures.

B Word Use
Write your own sentence using the underlined word in the sentence.

1 I'm tired of my monotonously **repetitive** daily life.

_____

2 The book is expected to **dominate** the best-seller lists.

_____

3 He **continually** studied and worked, without stopping to sleep.

_____

4 To use a military **analogy**, it was their Stalingrad.

_____

02 Presentation

Watch the presentation and answer the questions below.

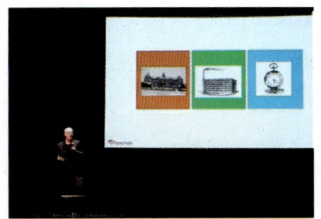

Gary Bolles talks about the shifts of society and the impact of the digital era to the current entrepreneurs. He explains the characteristics of work and suggests which skills to develop. He recommends how current entrepreneurs should behave in order to succeed within the modern society.

* Video may not be available depending on the connection to Youtube

A What's the presentation about?

_____
_____

B What's the purpose of this presentation?

_____
_____

C Summarize the story and present it to the class.

_____
_____
_____
_____
_____
_____

03 Transcript

Watch the presentation again and fill in the blanks with the words in the box.

Alright. How are you guys doing? I specialize in helping individuals and organizations to navigate (1)_____ change, I guess that connects to the earthquakes. And one of the biggest changes is the arc of our lives.

So nobody told you when you were in kindergarten that you were gonna have this big chunk of education, then this big chunk of work, then this big chunk of leisure in the period formerly known as retirement. And this construct came about back when we shifted from an agricultural to an industrial society. And we're going through this same type of shift to a digital society but in a blindingly short period of time. And the impact on a variety of different industries is that they're becoming unbundled.

So I used to work in the magazine business just like Quentin, along came the combination of technology and globalization, turned that on its side and blew it to bits, and as Quentin said, that's bad. So the result is that new players can come in and can dominate and so there's only one Amazon, one Facebook, and so on. And so this is affecting a wide range of different industries from the media business to transportation, and I believe that one of the next industries that's gonna become (2)_____, that's gonna become disrupted, is higher education.

Well why is this? It's because the arc of our lives is changing. And what's happening to industry after industry is that they've gone from healthy pyramids, that is small, niched, local, and focused, all the way up to big multinational organizations and everything in between and the combination of technology and globalization has (3)_____ the middle. That is, there aren't any more mid-sized companies. Only three tech companies have gone public this year. So what happens instead is what I call "the fat-bottomed world." There's a huge amount of innovation at the bottom where people can innovate and that's why we have so many start-ups, that's why we have so many incubators and (4)_____. It's because innovation is happening increasingly at the bottom.

I use the analogy of sea turtles. The mother sea turtle crawls up on the beach, she lays 10,000 eggs, the eggs hatch, they start to crawl down the beach and it's bugs, and sun, and birds…. And only a small percentage of those sea turtles actually reach the water. And so what we need is, we need to start to understand how we can adapt the way that we approach work and think differently so that more and more sea turtles can reach the water.

And so I use this disruptive change to talk about the underpinning as to why we work. What is work all about? What are jobs all about? I took this picture from the back of a bicycle when I was doing a lecture series for the New Zealand government. So the question as to why we work.

Well, let's understand what jobs are. We know from our work with a book called What Color Is Your Parachute, the world's most popular career manual with 10 million copies in print that there's seven different (5)_____. And because jobs are becoming unbundled, that is the combination of technology and globalization are breaking them apart.

I'm gonna focus specifically on the two most important things that you bring to the job. That's your skills, what you can do, and your knowledges, what you know. So why does somebody pay your for work? What is paid work? An employer or hirer has problems. They've got a series of challenges. They need tasks performed to solve each one of those problems and then you use what you know and what you can do to be able to perform those tasks. And increasingly this technology is taking a variety of different tasks, it's evaporating a bunch of the characteristics of what we thought of as jobs. So the message is not to slash our wrists, I'm actually gonna tell you this, a variety of different strategies to be able to adapt in these disruptive times.

I'm gonna give you four of them. So the first is that we need to focus more and more on developing the skills that use our brains, our creativity, and that are also unique tasks because it's the repetitive ones and the ones that take less (6)_____ that the robots and software are going to take down in the bottom corner. So we wanna move that magic quadrant. It turns out this also maps to the skills that you love and that you're really good at because we're trial-and-error machines. We'll keep on trying over and over again if we're using the skills that we enjoy using the most. So it's really, really important that we also think about the way that we turn that three boxes model on its side and we start to think of ourselves as lifelong learners, lifelong workers, and as Jenna was saying lifelong play as well, and be (7)_____ about it.

The fourth strategy is what I call a portfolio of work. Everything from a day job to working on your start-up on the side, more and more entrepreneurial thinking as to how we're continually floating, to be able to create value, and to find new opportunities to be able to solve problems.

So our opportunity, I'm not too worried about all of you in Silicon Valley because you're entrepreneurial thinkers. It's important that you also help others to think entrepreneurially. And if we change a lot of the underpinnings of our education system, of the way that we have (8)_____ environments for work, we can not only help ourselves to be able to navigate disruptive times, but to help others to thrive. Thanks.

07 Exercise

A Underline the best word to complete each sentence.

1 The latest computers can work at (blindingly / blindfold) fast speeds.

2 See the user's (manuscript / manual) on the website for details.

B Fill in the blanks with the given words.

| • quadrant | • evaporating | • continually |
| • disrupted | • proactive | • repetitive |

1 If the conversation becomes _____, they get bored easily.

2 Extreme weather patterns are caused by water _____ off of increasingly warm oceans.

3 The fragile balance of Earth's ecosystem is being _____.

4 To make matters worse, not many Western countries have been _____ toward accepting refugees.

C Fill in the blanks with the given words.

- accur every year
- a series of
- blown to bits
- to break the national team apart

1 More and more school shootings _____.

2 His car was completely _____ in the explosion, leaving almost nothing.

3 Despite their international success, the infighting is threatening _____.

4 _____ yellow arrows pointed the way to the reception.

Answer Key

Answer Key

Unit 01 Starting the Presentation

01 Vocabulary
A 1. yields 2. encouraging 3. tentative 4. preliminary

03 Presentation (1)
C 1. Welcome to 2. made it 3. start off on site

06 Mr. Q's Presentation
1. a 2. d

07 Exercise
A 1. overview 2. on site
B 1. encouraging 2. brief 3. company-wide 4. start off
C 1. have transformed the market fundamentally.
   2. in its preliminary stage.
   3. is essential when delivering a speech.
   4. on such short notice.

Unit 02 Engaging the Audience

01 Vocabulary
A 1. breakthrough 2. plausible 3. sampled 4. tantalizing

03 Presentation (1)
C 1. introduced 2. familiar 3. revolutionary 4. without

06 Mr. Q's Presentation
1. c 2. b

07 Exercise
A 1. transform 2. brew
B 1. indulge 2. tantalizing 3. plausible 4. breakthrough
C 1. This program will be of particular interest
   2. you'll be familiar with
   3. changing the entire industry
   4. Words alone cannot express

Unit 03 Stating the Purpose

01 Vocabulary
A 1. refrain 2. fundamental 3. noncontroversial 4. ardent

03 Presentation (1)
C 1. morality 2. hopefully 3. implications 4. potential

06 Mr. Q's Presentation
1. d 2. c

07 Exercise
A 1. come 2. fundamental
B 1. refrain 2. unfold 3. ardent 4. objective
C 1. If there is something I should know about,
   2. it is our mission to encourage
   3. This won't take more than half an hour
   4. This presentation will outline

Unit 04 Outlining

01 Vocabulary
A 1. pertinent 2. vast 3. aggressive 4. redefine

03 Presentation (1)
C 1. spread 2. divided 3. innovative 4. aside

06 Mr. Q's Presentation
1. b 2. c

07 Exercise
A 1. focus 2. aggressive
B 1. redefine 2. triple 3. pertinent 4. remarkable
C 1. please keep your questions to the end.
   2. Point one deals with the shoplifting issue,
   3. to focus on the details.
   4. go into more detail about

Unit 05 Actual Case 1

01 Vocabulary
A 1. prevalent 2. diabetes 3. obligation 4. doable

03 Transcript
1. prevalent 2. smoking 3. convince 4. interaction
5. obligations 6. reflective 7. opposition 8. bottom

07 Exercise
A 1. bottom 2. occur
B 1. prevalent 2. viable 3. convince 4. fluorescent

160 **BUSINESS INTERACTION** *Presentation*

C 1. think out of the box.
   2. come at the cost of
   3. have an obligation to
   4. is directly tied to

Unit 06 Analyzing

01 Vocabulary
A 1. exponential 2. accumulate 3. dwarf
   4. unforgiving

03 Presentation (1)
C 1. compares 2. dwarfed 3. gigantic 4. bunch

06 Mr. Q's Presentation
1. b   2. c

07 Exercise
A 1. continuous 2. leveling
B 1. exponential 2. dwarfed 3. sheer 4. accumulated
C 1. to turn things around in less than six months.
   2. hit their highest point last month
   3. grab market share in the coming years.
   4. while Korea tops the list.

Unit 07 Making Comparisons

01 Vocabulary
A 1. distinct 2. compromise 3. detrimental
   4. significant

03 Presentation (1)
C 1. consistently 2. compromises 3. comparison
   4. boast

06 Mr. Q's Presentation
1. d   2. a

07 Exercise
A 1. steady 2. similarities
B 1. distinct 2. detrimental 3. forecasts 4. significant
C 1. about the same as our competitor's.
   2. in comparison with those of China.
   3. when comparing the Greek economy
   4. This research is based on data

Unit 08 Making Contrasts

01 Vocabulary
A 1. copycats 2. marginal 3. tendency 4. volatile

03 Presentation (1)
C 1. exceptional 2. catch up 3. improvements
   4. achievement

06 Mr. Q's Presentation
1. d   2. b

07 Exercise
A 1. marginal 2. contrast
B 1. tendency 2. copycat 3. end users 4. volatile
C 1. in a number of important ways
   2. On the other hand
   3. more than twice as
   4. As a matter of fact

Unit 09 Emphasizing

01 Vocabulary
A 1. instrumental 2. reflection 3. instill 4. tremendous

03 Presentation (1)
C 1. exceptional 2. initiated 3. spotlight 4. stress

06 Mr. Q's Presentation
1. b   2. c

07 Exercise
A 1. critical 2. point
B 1. instill 2. drives 3. tremendous 4. instrumental
C 1. stress the importance of
   2. are a reflection of
   3. is essential to us is
   4. will put the spotlight on

Unit 10 Actual Case 2

01 Vocabulary
A 1. assess 2. automate 3. outperform 4. disparate

Answer Key

03 Transcript
1. dramatically 2. disruption 3. mimic 4. breakthroughs
5. outperform 6. disparate 7. reducible 8. shrink

04 Exercise
A 1. artificial 2. frequent
B 1. mimic 2. diagnose 3. disparate 4. breakthrough
C 1. have a higher risk of
   2. bring people together.
   3. have no chance of
   4. the extent of the damage

Unit 11 Introducing Visuals

01 Vocabulary
A 1. understating 2. shrank 3. adopted 4. crafted

03 Presentation (1)
C 1. demonstrates 2. permanent 3. contracts
   4. understates

06 Mr. Q's Presentation
1. a 2. b

07 Exercise
A 1. closer 2. demonstrates
B 1. stood 2. understate 3. spilled 4. adopt
C 1. on the bottom right hand corner
   2. marked in white
   3. To illustrate this
   4. put an updated contract list

Unit 12 Describing a Bar Graph

01 Vocabulary
A 1. prestige 2. enhance 3. depict 4. excelled

03 Presentation (1)
C 1. deals 2. compared 3. scrutiny 4. Simply

06 Mr. Q's Presentation
1. c 2. c

07 Exercise
A 1. excelled 2. falling
B 1. enhance 2. depict 3. prestige 4. apparent
C 1. illustrated in this bar graph
   2. deals with Citigroup's revenue
   3. it can be seen that
   4. far outweigh the costs

Unit 12 Describing a Bar Graph

01 Vocabulary
A 1. prestige 2. enhance 3. depict 4. excelled

03 Presentation (1)
C 1. deals 2. compared 3. scrutiny 4. Simply

06 Mr. Q's Presentation
1. c 2. c

07 Exercise
A 1. excelled 2. falling
B 1. enhance 2. depict 3. prestige 4. apparent
C 1. illustrated in this bar graph
   2. deals with Citigroup's revenue
   3. it can be seen that
   4. far outweigh the costs

Unit 13 Describing a Line Graph

01 Vocabulary
A 1. straightforward 2. obscure 3. disconcerting
   4. turnover

03 Presentation (1)
C 1. shortfall 2. balanced 3. fluctuates 4. essence

06 Mr. Q's Presentation
1. a 2. b

07 Exercise
A 1. witnessed 2. led
B 1. obscure 2. disconcerting 3. depiction 4. turnover
C 1. The first graph illustrates
   2. declined drastically after
   3. to be one of the contributing factors
   4. is likely to fluctuate in some way

Unit 14 Describing a Pie Chart

01 Vocabulary
A 1. deficit 2. recession 3. remaining 4. implemented

03 Presentation (1)
C 1. accounts 2. compare 3. revenue 4. recession

06 Mr. Q's Presentation
1. a   2. c

07 Exercise
A 1. bring 2. remaining
B 1. implement 2. deficit 3. standing 4. sound
C 1. comes in at second place
   2. accounted for two-thirds of
   3. are about three times higher
   4. were rounded off to

Unit 15 Actual Case 3

01 Vocabulary
A 1. voracious 2. misconception 3. whimsical
   4. facelift

03 Transcript
1. appetite 2. commercial 3. absorb 4. genuine
5. cornerstone 6. leverage 7. approachable
8. campaign

07 Exercise
A 1. extension 2. misconception
B 1. nostalgic 2. absorb 3. diversity 4. inspired
C 1. on our hands
   2. is such a big part of
   3. was the perfect way to
   4. to drum up our business

Unit 16 Highlighting Information

01 Vocabulary
A 1. functionality 2. sectors 3. accredited 4. boasts

03 Presentation (1)
C 1. point 2. bet 3. unctionality 4. expected

06 Mr. Q's Presentation
1. d   2. b

07 Exercise
A 1. doubt 2. in mind
B 1. functionality 2. boasts 3. sources 4. accredited
C 1. often overlooked in a debate
   2. can get a feel for
   3. The first thing to remember when
   4. We have to ask ourselves

Unit 17 Summarizing the Main Points

01 Vocabulary
A 1. progressive 2. Merely 3. pledged 4. favored

03 Presentation (1)
C 1. summarizing 2. diversity 3. progressive
   4. considered

06 Mr. Q's Presentation
1. b   2. a

07 Exercise
A 1. Merely 2. force
B 1. pledged 2. progressive 3. favored 4. concluded
C 1. In order to achieve our goals
   2. You have just learned
   3. On the whole
   4. Let me quickly run through

Unit 18 Closing a Presentation

01 Vocabulary
A 1. dedication 2. attained 3. endeavors 4. command

03 Presentation (1)
C 1. close 2. affected 3. simpler 4. ecommend

06 Mr. Q's Presentation
1. c   2. b

Answer Key

07 Exercise
A 1. downward 2. tough
B 1. endeavors 2. attained 3. convinced 4. command
C 1. I strongly recommend that
   2. Thank you for the hard work and dedication
   3. Let me bring my presentation to a close
   4. Mark my words, please

Unit 19 Handling the Q&A Session

01 Vocabulary
A 1. rephrases 2. resentment 3. bonanza
   4. undertaking

03 Presentation (1)
C 1. wrap up 2. cover 3. move on 4. urther

06 Mr. Q's Presentation
1. e   2. d

07 Exercise
A 1. rest 2. hidden
B 1. resentment 2. rephrase 3. fire away
   4. carte blanche
C 1. we are not in a position
   2. we are going to cover every aspect of
   3. broken down into two extreme ends
   4. Do you have any questions

07 Exercise
A 1. blindingly 2. manual
B 1. repetitive 2. evaporating 3. disrupted
   4. proactive
C 1. come about every year
   2. blown to bits
   3. to break the national team apart
   4. A series of

Unit 20 Actual Case 4

01 Vocabulary
A 1. seismic 2. disrupt 3. bonanza
   4. undertaking

03 Presentation (1)
C 1. wrap up 2. cover 3. evaporating 4. proactive

03 Transcript
1. seismic 2. unbundled 3. evaporated
4. accelerators 5. components 6. analytics
7. proactive 8. flexible

POCKET CAMPUS

원하는 강의만 골라 담자! 들고 다니는 나만의 캠퍼스

▶ 학습과정

외국어는 물론, 학습자들이 글로벌 시대에 갖춰야 할 취업, 인문학, IT, 리더십 등 다양한 지식을 쌓는 캠퍼스로 성장 할 것입니다.

    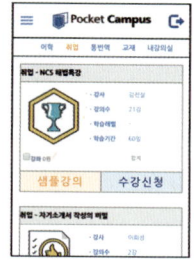 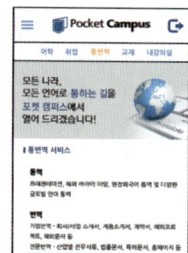

▶ Pocket Campus의 특징

· 합리적인 가격
강좌당 1만원 안팎의 저렴한 비용으로 학습하실 수 있습니다. 또한 원하는 과정을 장바구니에 담아 자신만의 강좌를 들을 수 있습니다.

· 다양한 커리큘럼
HiEnglish 전용교재를 학습할 수 있도록 자체 개발한 모바일 강의이기에 교재와 함께 학습하기에 최적화 되어 있습니다.

· 부담없는 학습분량
한 강좌에 15분 정도 분량이기 때문에 수업에 대한 부담이 없습니다. 동영상 강의를 듣는 학습자들의 학습패턴을 분석하여 적당한 학습 분량을 나누어 구성하였습니다.

 HiEnglish 모바일 학습사이트 포켓캠퍼스   www.pocketcampus.co.kr

자동 영문 이력서 작성, 영어 인터뷰 연습

Hi Sume

국내최초! 외국계 취업, 대기업 영어 면접, 해외 취업을 준비하는 분을 위한 자동 영문 이력서, 영어 인터뷰 연습을 돕는 "HiSume(하주메)" 어플 탄생!

동영상 강의

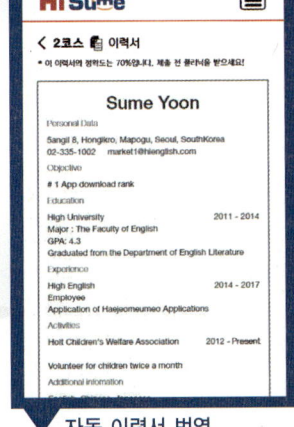
자동 이력서 번역

영어 인터뷰 연습

다양한 서비스

HiSume 는 이런 사람들에게 필요합니다.

✓ 외국계 기업 취직을 준비중인 분
✓ 대기업 영어 인터뷰를 준비중인 분
✓ 해외 취업이나 유학을 준비중인 분

👍 하주메(HiSume) 무료 서비스

· 주요 외국계 기업 영어 인터뷰 기출 문제 음성 수록
· 국문 이력서와 커버레터를 영문으로 자동 번역
· 영어 인터뷰 답변 녹음 및 정답확인
· 영문 이력서, 커버레터, 영어 인터뷰 등 동영상 강의

🎖 하주메(HiSume) 유료 서비스

· 원어민 및 전현직 인사담당자의 이력서, 커버레터 첨삭 지도
· 1:1 영어 인터뷰 코칭

하주메 어플 무료로 다운 받는 법!
구글 플레이스토어 에서 '하주메(HiSume)'를 검색 하거나, 하단에 QR코드를 찍는다.

하이유니 홈페이지 www.hiuni.co.kr 전화 070-7169-0708
메일문의 unv3@hiuni.co.kr , market1@hienglish.com